T0312270

Cambridge Elements

Elements in Poetry and Poetics
edited by
Eric Falci
University of California, Berkeley

RADICAL TENDERNESS

Poetry in Times of Catastrophe

Andrea Brady
Queen Mary University of London

CAMBRIDGE
UNIVERSITY PRESS

CAMBRIDGE
UNIVERSITY PRESS

Shaftesbury Road, Cambridge CB2 8EA, United Kingdom

One Liberty Plaza, 20th Floor, New York, NY 10006, USA

477 Williamstown Road, Port Melbourne, VIC 3207, Australia

314–321, 3rd Floor, Plot 3, Splendor Forum, Jasola District Centre, New Delhi – 110025, India

103 Penang Road, #05–06/07, Visioncrest Commercial, Singapore 238467

Cambridge University Press is part of Cambridge University Press & Assessment, a department of the University of Cambridge.

We share the University's mission to contribute to society through the pursuit of education, learning and research at the highest international levels of excellence.

www.cambridge.org
Information on this title: www.cambridge.org/9781009517331

DOI: 10.1017/9781009393430

First published 2024

A catalogue record for this publication is available from the British Library.

ISBN 978-1-009-51733-1 Hardback
ISBN 978-1-009-39344-7 Paperback
ISSN 2752-5236 (online)
ISSN 2752-5228 (print)

Cambridge University Press & Assessment has no responsibility for the persistence or accuracy of URLs for external or third-party internet websites referred to in this publication and does not guarantee that any content on such websites is, or will remain, accurate or appropriate.

Radical Tenderness

Poetry in Times of Catastrophe

Elements in Poetry and Poetics

DOI: 10.1017/9781009393430
First published online: April 2024

Andrea Brady
Queen Mary University of London
Author for correspondence: Andrea Brady, a.brady@qmul.ac.uk

Abstract: *Radical Tenderness* argues for the importance of poetry in negotiating political and social catastrophes through a focus on the unusual intimacies of committed writing. How do poets negotiate between the personal and the public, the bedroom and the street, the family and class or communal ties? How does contemporary lyric, with its emphasis on the feelings and perceptions of the individual subject, speak to moments of shared crisis? What can poetry tell us about how care shapes our experiences of history? How do the intimacies found in protest, on strike, in riots, and in spaces of oppression transform individual lives and political movements? Through a series of focussed readings of four twenty-first-century poets – Caleb Femi, Bhanu Kapil, Juliana Spahr, and Anne Boyer – *Radical Tenderness* reflects the perspectives provided by intimate poetries on the shared political emergencies of poverty, war, ecological catastrophe, racism, and illness.

This Element also has a video abstract: www.cambridge.org/radicaltenderness

Keywords: poetry, poetics, politics, race, Illness

ISBNs: 9781009517331 (HB), 9781009393447 (PB), 9781009393430 (OC)
ISSNs: 2752-5236 (online), 2752-5228 (print)

Contents

Introduction

This Element considers four different examples of lyric intimacy, but not the usual kind. The poems by Caleb Femi, Bhanu Kapil, Juliana Spahr, and Anne Boyer discussed in these sections seek out the radical tenderness that emerges in political struggle: new relations that open out beyond the privacy of the couple form into the intimacies discoverable in moments of intense public crisis. Such openings expand the practice of poetic writing beyond the production of diminished relics of archaic abundance or socially valueless forms, aligning with a history of lyric dominated not by individual sentiment, inaction, and self-address but by collective experience, political organising, and attention to the shared traumas and possibilities of political life.

The antithetical approaches to lyric caricatured in that last sentence seem to be a legacy of Romanticism, or rather, that antithesis recapitulates a version of Romanticism against which much contemporary experimental poetry has pitched itself.[1] Virginia Jackson and Yopie Prins have argued that a process of 'lyricisation', which began in the eighteenth century, caused the ancient plurality of poetic genres to collapse into the scarcity of lyric.[2] As lyric became nearly synonymous with poetry, poetry became an art form centred on a sensitive poetic 'I' capable of incorporating history into its authenticated privacies. Jonathan Culler has debated some of these claims, contending that lyric is a ritual with a special temporality that foregrounds presentness, and a pliant genre whose history goes much further back than Prins and Jackson allege.[3] These arguments have preoccupied what is known as 'New Lyric Studies' in recent years, a controversy that has also been critiqued for its whiteness by a number of scholars.[4] This Introduction won't rehash such disputes, but they are an indication of the resurgence of lyric as an object of praise and suspicion in contemporary literary criticism, long after its premature obsolescence was declared by some factions of the poetry avant-garde. Here, I will simply establish a few headings under which this short book's analysis of lyric collectivities will be gathered: the inward

---

[1] On the caricaturing of Romantic lyric within lyric theory, see Madeleine Callaghan, 'What Can the Romantic Lyric Do?', *Textual Practice* 37.12 (2023): 1981–1999.

[2] Virginia Jackson, *Dickinson's Misery: A Theory of Lyric Reading* (Princeton, NJ: Princeton University Press, 2005); Virginia Jackson and Yopie Prins (eds.), *The Lyric Theory Reader: A Critical Anthology* (Baltimore, MD: Johns Hopkins University Press, 2014).

[3] Jonathan Culler, 'Why Lyric?', *PMLA* 123.1 (January 2008): 201–206.

[4] Dorothy J. Wang, *Thinking Its Presence: Form, Race, and Subjectivity in Contemporary Asian American Poetry* (Stanford, CA: Stanford University Press, 2013), 1–48; Sarah Dowling, *Translingual Poetics: Writing Personhood Under Settler Colonialism* (Iowa City, IA: University of Iowa Press, 2018), 59; Jahan Ramazani, 'Poetry and Race: An Introduction', *New Literary History* 50.4 (Autumn 2019), vii–xxxvii (x).

turn towards the lyric 'I' ('yeh, that thing'),[5] *poiesis* and crisis, intimacy and tenderness, personal and social or revolutionary love.

Radical Tenderness argues that there are contemporary poets who remain keen to repurpose the conventions of lyric to imagine new kinds of relatedness for which there is no, or insufficient, language: to give, in Audre Lorde's endlessly useful formulation, 'a name to the nameless so that it can be thought'.[6] Drawing on lyric's ancient association with loss and ruin,[7] these poems speak tenderly for and with the 'we' that forms in emergencies of many different kinds – environmental disaster, war, illness, poverty, precarity in all its intersectional forms – while edging very carefully around the authority and exclusivity of that awkward pronoun. If they are on any front line, it is the (broken) line where new vocabularies emerge from shared emergencies, calling for help and attention. As such, they can help us to imagine ways out of crisis through solidarities of languages, practices, and bodies.

Lyric Inwardness

In the supposedly Romantic tradition, lyric is valued for its ability to compound the cipher of the individual into a figure of universal truth. A key figure in these arguments is G.W.F. Hegel, who in his lectures on aesthetics proposed that the lyric poet 'absorbs into himself the entire world of objects and circumstances and stamps them with his own inner consciousness'.[8] In lyric, 'the language of the poetic inner life' comes to 'possess a universal validity' and transcend the individual. Assimilating into his own creativity and 'rich inner life' the objective reality of his history and nation, the poet makes 'something universally human' of his feelings and experiences (1121). Unburdened by the abstractions that haunt the philosopher, the poet's outpourings of soul are nonetheless disturbing, forcing him to accept his 'particularisation and individualisation' (1132) where the philosopher can find peace in the universality of his discoveries.

But the historical affordances of the lyric 'I' are distributed unequally. Not every lyric subject can lay claim easily to universal validity, not least because not all lyric subjects have historically been regarded as equally human. Sandeep Parmar notes the 'inherent premise of universality' in lyric is connected to its

---

[5] Sean Bonney, *Letters against the Firmament* (London: Enitharmon, 2015), 142.
[6] Audre Lorde, 'Poetry Is Not a Luxury' (1977), in *Sister Outsider: Essays and Speeches*, ed. Nancy K. Bereano (Berkeley, CA: Crossing Press, 2007), 37.
[7] 'When I use the word *human*, I think of it as implicitly asking a question. What alternative genres can it name? For me, the lyric asks the same question because it, too, like the idea of the human, is founded in ruin.' Min Hyoung Song, *Climate Lyricism* (Durham, NC: Duke University Press, 2022), 55.
[8] Georg Wilhelm Friedrich Hegel, *Aesthetics: Lectures on Fine Art*, trans. T. M. Knox, 2 vols. (Oxford: Clarendon Press, 1975 [1988]), 2:1111.

'coded whiteness', asking: 'How do poets of colour themselves differently embody the 'I'? Or does it come to embody us? Is it no more than the dead metaphor of our failed universality, of our being as other?'[9] The question is echoed by Dorothy Wang: 'How does one begin writing when the "I" who speaks emanates from a body that is viewed a priori as a not-citizen, a not-person, a not-human? How to write when the "I" can not contain the fragments shattered by dislocation, emigration, immigration, and assimilation?'[10] Wang is interested in the 'pathologized "I" – not the universal speaker but the unloved speaker' (84). Unloved lyric subjects who want to be met 'halfway' across the borders of states and properties will appear in the poetics of several of these writers.

While critics, including Wang, have emphasised the whiteness of the fiction of a universalising lyric 'I', that fiction continues (in the form of Michael Gove's revisionist curriculum) to menace British schoolchildren.[11] It is not hard to guess why a declining post-imperial nation would wish to assure its subjects that Anglophone poetry transcends its small particularity and lays claim to the whole territory of the human condition. Nonetheless, the idea that poetry communicates timeless truths gleaned by a perceptive individual seems to serve an unmet need for many readers – a need, perhaps, for assurance that our experiences are not ruthlessly conditional. That need should be taken seriously. Once the aim of universalising or the faith in universality is lost, all that's left is the cipher, which restricts the capacity of modern poetry to speak to, for, or with its community in the way that epic and oral poetries do. Instead, lyric becomes a niche cultural form, its producers pickling in inescapable negation.

Sharpening Hegel's arguments for the transcendence of lyric particularity, Theodor Adorno argues that 'lyric work is always the subjective expression of a social antagonism'.[12] Lyric catches in its dialectical formality the opposition

---

[9] Sandeep Parmar with Bhanu Kapil, 'Lyric Violence, the Nomadic Subject and the Fourth Space', in *Threads* (London: Clinic, 2018), 11. Parmar's argument that 'the lyric "I" that interests me here will be familiar: it emerges from Romanticism – and averts its eyes during modernism – to find itself contemporarily suspended in the epiphanic present of the poetic anecdote. Its border guards are the literary gatekeepers of shared assumptions about experience, language and tradition' is highly relevant to this discussion (10).

[10] Dorothy Wang, 'Speculative Notes on Bhanu Kapil', in *Nests and Strangers: On Asian American Women Poets*, ed. Timothy Yu (Berkeley, CA: Kelsey Street Press, 2015), 78–91 (78).

[11] 'Literary texts are a reflection of, and exploration of, the human condition, the study of which develops empathic understanding of human nature. High-quality English literature is writing that displays recognisable literary qualities and, although shaped by particular contexts, transcends them and speaks about the universality of the human condition.' AQA Mark Scheme, English Literature paper 8702/1P, June 2022: https://filestore.aqa.org.uk/sample-papers-and-mark-schemes/2022/june/AQA-87021P-MS-JUN22.PDF.

[12] Theodor Adorno, 'On Lyric Poetry and Society', in *Notes to Literature*, vol. 1, trans. Shierry Weber Nicholsen (New York, NY: Columbia University Press, 1991), 37–54 (45).

between the subjective and the objective, the falsities of social life and 'something not distorted, not grasped, not yet subsumed' (38), something whole and self-determining: a possibility of freedom beyond alienation. It does so through the crux of the individual subject, even though that individual is also the product of capitalist developments that make freedom nearly impossible. For Adorno, 'the lyric work hopes to attain universality through unrestrained individuation' (38). This hope is realised through aesthetic form, rather than any direct commentary on social conditions, which are manifested instead as 'an accord with language itself' (43) – language speaking with the subject's voice. These are historical processes: the lyric that protests against its conditions by withdrawing into inwardness is consummately bourgeois, the lyric 'I' it propagates 'something opposed to the collective, to objectivity' (41). But even bourgeois lyric's 'withdrawal into itself, its self-absorption, its detachment from the social surface, is socially motivated behind the author's back' (43). There's no getting away from the contradictions. While Adorno would likely find the poetries discussed in this Element too programmatic, they all begin with social antagonism and reach towards the reconciliation of subject with objective reality. In their critiques of racialisation, global supply chains, and settler colonialism, they also attend explicitly to the universal, here known as the edgeless 'electrified grid' that is capitalism. Their lyric subjects are fractured things, caught in these historical processes, but are unable or unwilling to turn their back on struggle, sustaining themselves with riot and song.

Withdrawal and self-absorption are, as Adorno makes clear, historical and ideological processes, not timeless qualities of poetry. This point is not always sufficiently emphasised in writings about the category of the lyric. Tilottama Rajan observes that in Romantic poetry, 'lyricisation had signified internalisation, a retreat into a transcendental identity, and a certain idealism and resistance to materiality'; it meant the expectation of 'an ontopoetics of presence' and 'a suppression of temporality'.[13] This – following Sharon Cameron's work on lyric temporalities – 'has the effect of exempting the self from action, from involvement in the complex intertexture of events' (Rajan 12). Cameron herself argues that lyric is a compression machine: 'All time converges on the poem in whose one space splintered temporal fragments lodge and totalise. The poem lifts the fragments out of a severative reality. It prolongs, exaggerates, speeds up, subordinates, and, simultaneously, seals its moments off from the world.'[14] Lyric form in Cameron's terms marks a separation from the world, the moment

---

[13] Tilottama Rajan, *Romantic Narrative* (Baltimore, MD: Johns Hopkins University Press, 2010), xii.

[14] Sharon Cameron, *Lyric Time: Emily Dickinson and the Limits of Genre* (Baltimore, MD: Johns Hopkins University Press, 1979), 258.

sealed in an airtight container of presentness, the self suspended motionless within it. The poem's value emerges from such hermetic temporality, which resists equivalencies and is absolutely opposed to socially necessary labour time. But who, living a life of splintered temporal fragments in which the speed of production is not measurable as prosody, has the time to write or read it?

For Rajan, lyric's inward turn is a consequence of both its form and its veneration of subjective experience in the absence of a reader – or as Jerome McGann puts it, that reader's indifference, which makes it seem as if the writer is 'intent only on communing with his own soul'. The poet turns his back on listeners, in Northrop Frye's well-known formulation, giving the social motivations space to operate.[15] These moves, familiar from the prison cell analogy of J. S. Mill, suggest that lyric's passion for intimacy crystallises present contingencies as eternal verities at the expense of the world.[16] But as Walt Hunter argues, lyricisation was ideological from the outset: 'The very idea of a bourgeois lyric subject is made possible by the existence of a (lyric) object: the commodified human, the Atlantic slave trade, and the ongoing racialised violence necessary for the continuation of capitalism.'[17] And withdrawal is a luxury not given to everyone. Kamran Javadizadeh asks: 'Once the idea of a transcendent lyric subject – the end result of a century and a half of lyricisation – has been exposed as a form of white innocence, how can a poet retain the intimacy allowed by the lyric tradition without replicating its pernicious political effects?'[18] The desire to retain intimacy while analysing or sequestering some of its effects can be found in different ways in all four poetries discussed in this Element, but so can the fear that there is no such thing as an inward turn anymore, no way of turning our backs on a world whose damage we cause and enjoy in our private spaces stuffed with things.

---

[15] Jerome McGann, 'Private Poetry, Public Deception', in *The Politics of Poetic Form*, ed. Charles Bernstein (New York, NY: Roof Books, 1990), 119–147 (123); Northrop Frye, *Anatomy of Criticism: Four Essays* (Toronto: University of Toronto Press, 2006), 231. The early modern history of lyric's inward turn is historicised by Anne Ferry, *The 'Inward' Language: Sonnets of Wyatt, Sidney, Shakespeare and Donne* (Chicago, IL: University of Chicago Press, 1983).

[16] John Stuart Mill, *Autobiography and Literary Essays*, ed. John M. Robson and Jack Stillinger (1981), vol. 1 of *The Collected Works of John Stuart Mill*, ed. John M Ronson et al., 33 vols. (University of Toronto Press and Routledge and Kegan Paul, 1963–1991), 37–9.

[17] Walt Hunter, *Forms of a World: Contemporary Poetry and the Making of Globalization* (New York, NY: Fordham University Press, 2019), 11.

[18] Kamran Javadizadeh, 'The Atlantic Ocean Breaking on Our Heads: Claudia Rankine, Robert Lowell, and the Whiteness of the Lyric Subject', *PMLA* 134.3 (2019): 475–490 (477). For an impressive reading of how the trope of apostrophe in nineteenth-century poetry encodes whiteness, and an engagement with Culler's prioritisation of that trope in his writing on lyric, see Virginia Jackson, 'Apostrophe, Animation, and Racism', *Critical Inquiry* 48.4 (2022): 652–675; the racialisation of apostrophe is also discussed in Hunter, 58–9.

Rajan argues that it is poetry, or *poiesis* in its Coleridgean form, which, 'as it "dissolves, diffuses and dissipates" forms in order to "re-create" them, gives us access to the structuring and destructuring processes at work in textual production' (xvi). This dissolution and recreation discloses the fantastic and chaotic energies at work within the public sphere, and reminds us – echoing Adorno – that 'poetry is part of the work of the negative' (Rajan xvi). But maybe what is at stake in *poiesis* is more than just textual production: it might also be the wish to participate in the dissolution and recreation of the world, a world that already seems to be disintegrating in front of our eyes. Poetry's making and unmaking is an analogue for the processes, but it also has the potential to imagine their alternative.

The poets discussed in these sections all share a sense of urgency about the need to remake the world, even if they differ in their sense of how this might be accomplished. While their published writings suggest that Spahr's orientation is broadly anarchist, anti-state and anti-capitalist, and Boyer's is broadly communist, Kapil's politics seem aligned with ecological, feminist, and anti-racist thought and praxis. Femi disavows the position of the 'political poet' in his interviews, while nonetheless enacting a class-conscious critique of white Britishness. He says, 'Being a political poet is dead. I don't subscribe to that, however, that doesn't stop the work I make from being political, because it is.'[19] Politics is defined by praxis, rather than theory, for him. But as Christopher Nealon has shown, 'it is not only the poetries of witness and documentation, or movement poetries, that are worrying over the destiny that capitalism is forcing us toward'; every poetry is political these days, perhaps especially those poetries that claim not to be. These poets offer a variety of aesthetic and political responses to Nealon's question of 'what poetry is, or would have to be, in order to be opposed to capital: equally substantial, or equally insubstantial? Fleet and circulatory, like money, or defiantly valueless, money's opposite? Imitative of the movements that produce crisis and rushing headlong into it, or built to survive crisis and live on into a postcapitalist future?'[20] To which I'd add: a parody of the family, or an extension of kinship? An elegy for concretisation, or a fantasy of abstraction? Individual, or collective? Sick, or well? Intimate, or public? The answer, in each case, is resolutely dialectical, embracing *poiesis* as both making and unmaking, mourning for and relishing the world that is, and welcoming the world that might be.

---

[19] ' Caleb Femi and Athian Akec in conversation', *Huck* (21 December 2020), www.huckmag.com/art-and-culture/caleb-femi-and-athian-akec-in-conversation/.

[20] Christopher Nealon, *The Matter of Capital: Poetry and Crisis in the American Century* (Cambridge, MA: Harvard University Press, 2011), 35, 30.

Intimacies without Canon

The poets discussed in this Element also make use of lyric's ambivalent relationship to intimacy. Lyricisation has centred intimacy as both a feeling and an emplacement: the tender address to the beloved, the reader, creating fictions of privacy and authenticity that resist the intrusions of the sovereign, while noticing everywhere the impressions of power. In lyric's 'interpersonal play between the I and you', the relational nature of the lyric subject emerges, and the space where 'interiority begins and exteriority ends' blurs, Min Hyoung Song argues.[21] The intimacy of direct address within the lyric I/thou relation clings to the reader also, and even in its most impersonal modes lyric draws out intimate entanglement of the speaker with the 'flesh of the world' (in Merleau-Ponty's phrase).[22]

Lauren Berlant's analysis of 'intimate publics' offers a more critical perspective on the function of intimacy. For Berlant, such publics are spaces where consumers '*already* share a worldview and emotional knowledge that they have derived from a broadly common historical experience'. By 'expressing the sensational, embodied experiences of living as a certain kind of being in the world', intimate publics promise 'a better experience of social belonging' – one achieved through shared identifications and sentimentality.[23] Mandem in Femi's poetry, or cancer patients in Boyer's recent work, are alternative examples of such intimate publics.

Lyric poetry is not an intimate public, though it's not not one either. Certainly, many contemporary poems foreground 'affective and emotional attachments located in fantasies of the common, the everyday, and a sense of ordinariness' (10). Berlant focuses on the conservative tendencies in women's commodified, sentimental culture; the observation that such culture dwells in the fantastic 'zone of stop-loss, a demand for the ongoing present to be the scene of lived fulfilment', rather than the 'serious' politics that 'risks a loss of the ground of living' (12), can also be applied to many poetries. Though poets often celebrate poetry's resistance to commodification (resolutely defending the poem's abject unsalability as a marker of authenticity, resistance, or aesthetic value), they do share fantasies 'of transcending, dissolving, or refunctioning the obstacles that shape their historical conditions' (8) – that dissolution being very close to Coleridge's definition of the poetic imagination as that which 'dissolves, diffuses, dissipates, in order to recreate: or where this process is rendered

---

[21] Song 42.

[22] Maurice Merleau-Ponty, *Nature: Course Notes from the Collège de France*, trans. Robert Vallier (Evanston, IL: Northwestern University Press, 2003), 216.

[23] Lauren Berlant, *The Female Complaint: The Unfinished Business of Sentimentality in American Culture* (Durham, NC: Duke University Press, 2008), viii.

impossible, yet still at all events it struggles to idealise and to unify'. Well, who wouldn't?

Berlant's work elaborates a range of enigmatic attachments and 'processes by which intimate lives absorb and repel the rhetorics, laws, ethics, and ideologies of the hegemonic public sphere, but also personalise the effects of the public sphere and reproduce a fantasy that private life is the real in contrast to collective life: the surreal, the elsewhere, the fallen, the irrelevant'. Intimacy, Berlant continues, 'poses a question of scale that links the instability of individual lives to the trajectories of the collective'.[24] Part of its utility for Berlant as a concept for thinking about contemporary life is the awkward resilience of intimacy and its pleasures and appetites within political domains whose commitment to rationality and universalism has supposedly banished the personal – though it's doubtful if such domains have ever actually existed. Berlant's interest in minor intimacies opens up the frustrations of expression that attend non-normative desires: 'desires for intimacy that bypass the couple or the life narrative it generates have no alternative plots, let alone few laws and stable spaces of culture in which to clarify and to cultivate them. What happens to the energy of attachment when it has no designated place? To the glances, gestures, encounters, collaborations, or fantasies that have no canon?' (285). Poetry is one place where those energies and expressions that have 'no canon' can become one: or if not canonical, can stretch the resources of language and the political imaginary by denaturalising social formations, such as gender or the love plot, holding in one frame a critique of the present and a longing, creative orientation towards the horizon of revolutionary possibility.[25] An expanded lyric intimacy, as in Spahr's work, might encompass 'desire, and conventional domestic relationships, and unconventional ones, and fucking, and friendships, and close momentary contact between strangers in urban areas, and identity and identification with those like and unlike'.[26] We could also begin to glimpse there our intimacies with more-than-human others, with environments and things.

Radical Tenderness

But this revised lyric intimacy will not serve a radical politics if it merely expands the domain of possessive individualism, underpinned by conventional

---

[24] Lauren Berlant, 'Intimacy', *Critical Inquiry* 24.2 (Winter 1998): 282–3.

[25] On poetry's capacity to denaturalise gender, see Amy De'Ath, 'Hidden Abodes and Inner Bonds: Literary Study and Marxist-Feminism', in *After Marx: Literature, Theory, and Value in the Twenty-First Century*, ed. Colleen Lye and Christopher Nealon (Cambridge: Cambridge University Press, 2022), 225–240.

[26] Juliana Spahr, '"Love Scattered, Not Concentrated Love": Bernadette Mayer's *Sonnets*', *Jacket* 7 (April 1999): http://jacketmagazine.com/07/spahr-mayer.html.

erotic and familial structures, to the animals, the soil, the urban stranger. So let's call it tenderness instead. While intimacy has been the subject of copious theorisation,[27] I've been drawn to the term radical tenderness since 2017, when it arose in a conversation I had with Andy Spragg for *Poetry London*. Spragg quoted John Berger, who said in conversation with Michael Silverblatt: 'It seems to me that one of the essential elements in tenderness is that it is a free act, a gratuitous act. It has an enormous amount to do with liberty, with freedom, because one chooses to be tender ... in the face of what surrounds us, it is an almost defiant act.'[28] That freedom and gratuity links tenderness to a long history of thinking about aesthetics. Berger sees the free choice of tenderness in a brutal world as defiance – a form of courage, but also a refusal of the terms of what exists. As Anne Boyer writes, 'Whatever exists in the relation of love against the relation of profit, whatever refuses a brand: this is the soul, the organ of refusal.'[29] It is a tender organ.

The term 'radical tenderness' has arisen in the work of other authors, including recently Şeyda Kurt.[30] In their 2015 manifesto on radical tenderness, the transfeminist activists Dani d'Emilia and Daniel B. Coleman highlight the festive, careful aspects of this quality. 'Radical tenderness is to be critical and loving, at the same time', they write.[31] In another iteration of the manifesto, d'Emilia and Vanessa Andreotti urge: 'Collectivise your heart so that it breaks open and not apart.' They emphasise 'co-sensing', attending specifically to the embodied aspects of radical action: 'Tend the wounds created when the skin holding one body stretches and tears in order to receive and be refigured by another.' The image is gestational: the activist is asked to 'assist with the birth of something new, without suffocating what is being born with projections and

---

[27] See, for example, Anthony Giddens, *The Transformation of Intimacy: Sexuality, Love, and Eroticism in Modern Societies* (Cambridge: Polity, 1992); 'Intimacy: A Special Issue', *Critical Inquiry* 24.2 (Winter 1998), and *Intimacy*, ed. Lauren Berlant (Chicago, IL: University of Chicago Press, 2000); Leo Bersani and Adam Phillips, *Intimacies* (Chicago, IL: University of Chicago Press, 2008); *Scenes of Intimacy: Reading, Writing, and Theorising Contemporary Literature*, ed. Jennifer Cooke (London: Bloomsbury Academic, 2013); and *Love and the Politics of Intimacy: Bodies, Boundaries, Liberation*, ed. Stanislava Dikova, Wendy McMahon, and Jordan Savage (London: Bloomsbury, 2023).

[28] Andy Spragg, 'On Radical Tenderness: Interview with Andrea Brady', *Poetry London* (1 February 2018). The interview with Berger can be viewed at www.youtube.com/watch? v=BLivFgw_i-8.

[29] Sam Jaffe Goldstein, 'Find Something to Hide as soon as Possible: An Interview with Anne Boyer', *The End of the World Review* (15 September 2020): https://endoftheworld.substack.com/p/find-something-to-hide-as-soon-as.

[30] Şeyda Kurt, *Radikale Zärtlichkeit: Warum Lieve Politisch Ist* (Berlin: Harper Collins, 2022).

[31] Dani d'Emilia and Daniel B. Coleman, 'Radical Tenderness Manifesto' (2015): https://danidemilia.com/radical-tenderness/.

idealizations'.[32] Tenderness clings to bodies, expanding their potential, even if it can be difficult to imagine a relatedness that is not, at least analogically, erotic or reproductive.

My use of the word 'tenderness' in the title of this Element wishes to remember the 'infantile and unmanly phenomena' that the noun has historically gathered in its keeping,[33] in opposition to heroic and hypermasculine visions of revolutionary action. In psychoanalysis, tenderness is a developmental stage that characterises the relation of the primary caregiver to the infant. Freud writes of *Zärtlichkeit* ('the affectionate current') that it 'springs from the earliest years of childhood; it is formed on the basis of the interests of the self-preservative instinct and is directed to the members of the family and those who look after the child'; and while it 'carries along with it contributions from the sexual instincts' from the beginning, it is subsumed in puberty by a 'sensual current' that translates these early experiences from the primary object choice (the mother) to other objects. Or at least that's how it should work; the failure to make clear distinctions between incestuous mother-love and appropriate other-love leads to impotence, or idealisation, such that 'Where they love they do not desire and where they desire they cannot love.'[34] The inability to establish the correct 'confluence' between affection and sensuality cleaves the object into two: one debased and the other idealised, the wrecked world and the transfigured. But the stage of tenderness is also one of great vulnerability. Writing of his treatment of patients who had been sexually abused in childhood, Ferenczi notes the potential for pathological consequences if '*more love* or *love of a different kind from that which they need*' is forced upon children in the stage of tenderness; for 'they cannot do without tenderness, especially that which comes from the mother'.[35]

Associated in psychoanalysis with maternal care, tenderness gives way to, and extends beyond, desire. It is the primal instance of intimacy but can be offered without intimacy. It is a form of care that preserves the organism and creates social bonds, though perverted, it can lead to great destructiveness. It is a form of attention to the needs of the other. Its haptic quality implies lightness and contact, a gentle approach to the boundaries of the other that is not

---

[32] Dani d'Emilia, Vanessa Andreotti and GTDF Collective, 'Co-sensing with Radical Tenderness': https://decolonialfutures.net/rt-recording/.

[33] Gavin Miller, 'A Wall of Ideas: The "Taboo on Tenderness" in Theory and Culture', *New Literary History* 38.4 (Autumn, 2007): 667–681 (675).

[34] Sigmund Freud, 'On the Universal Tendency to Debasement in the Sphere of Love', in *Standard Edition of the Complete Psychological Works*, vol. 11 (1910), ed. James Strachey (London: Vintage, 2011), 177–190 (180–1, 183).

[35] Sándor Ferenczi, 'Confusion of Tongues between Adults and the Child' (1933), in *Final Contributions to the Problems and Methods of Psychoanalysis*, ed. Michael Balint, trans. Eric Mosbacher et al. (London: Routledge, 2018), 156–167 (164).

demanding or acquisitive. It is also a legacy of woundedness, of the flesh that has been pummelled and is now soft enough to eat. It is related to natality, but we can agree to release the concept from its links to reproductive futurism and think instead of tenderness as a way of nurturing new forms of being together. It is a mode of caring that sets itself up eventually to be outmoded. But we cannot do without it.

Conceptually, tenderness is less encumbered than love. Elizabeth Povinelli has argued that love – for all its promise to produce a 'rupture' from the old self and the world that produces that self – is key to the emergence of liberal notions of individual autonomy, 'stitching the rhythms of politics and the market to the rhythms of the intimate subject'. This is a seam explored by the poets in this Element. But at its best, the ruptures in subjectivity that love promises also lead us to 'reform the social', making the social 'appear as a form of bondage, mere surface or impasse'.[36] For writers of lyric, a genre saturated in personal love, finding a way to break the synchronicity of the rhythms of the self and the market requires experiments with grammar, syntax, form, and lineation: trespasses into prose, fading affect into flat style, wrong pronouns, the performance of passivity, or ironic overinvestments in traditional couple forms. As will be seen, three of these poets write in combinations of poetry and prose; but while the poem, Giorgio Agamben instructs us, is defined by its ability through lineation and enjambment to oppose a metrical limit to a syntactical limit, I will take these writers' self-identification as poets and the complex specificities of their language use as justification for considering their work as poetry.[37] Their formal and aesthetic experiments are presented as experiments for living, imagining ways to move tenderly through personal love towards social love.

Social Love

Poets are, of course, not the only activists imagining alternative plots and encounters, ways of outwitting erotic and kin-based forms of privacy (or privation) in pursuit of new relations. For Joy James, revolutionary *poiesis* is driven by desire – whether for justice, survival, or the flourishing of others. James defends 'Revolutionary Love' as a force sustained by political will 'even when one wishes its dissipation or dissolution in order to dodge the

---

[36] Elizabeth A. Povinelli, *The Empire of Love: Toward a Theory of Intimacy, Genealogy, and Carnality* (Durham, NC: Duke University Press, 2006), 190–1.

[37] Giorgio Agamben, *The End of the Poem: Studies in Poetics*, trans. Daniel Heller-Roazen (Stanford, CA: Stanford University Press, 1999), 109.

entanglements and suffering of liberation struggles'.[38] Revolutionary love is 'tangible, not mystical … [It] transcends the family, the personal partner or partners, the self-love or self-loathing … It is that love of us collectively, and the better us, and the right to live without extraction and exploitation and intimidation' (291). Working to dissolve both the ego and the state in the struggle, the activist in James's view embraces a negativity that demands the abolition of the privileges of individuality. This is a challenge for the lyric as a form that is strongly associated with those privileges. As Jasper Bernes, Juliana Spahr and Joshua Clover have written, 'The vocation of the poet becomes self-destruction; the vocation of the poem, self-abolition.'[39] The liberation struggle demands new lyrics.

Sophie Lewis, in her manifesto *Abolish the Family*, offers a definition of love that is aligned with James's revolutionary love: 'To love a person is to struggle for their autonomy as well as for their immersion in care, insofar as such abundance is possible in a world choked by capital.'[40] Love is more than what the poets claim for their mistresses. It is a political action directed towards magnifying the possibility for unalienated being in the world. But as things are, 'Love is locked up', as Lola Olufemi writes:

> Love continues to be crushed by
> RIGHT NOW, by the prison, by cycles of dispossession.
> It is only as grand as the world allows it to be[41]

Love is choked, Lewis agrees: '*caring, sharing, and loving* are at present to be sought, depended upon, and expected pretty much *only* in kinship contexts. This amounts to a tragic, intricate orchestration of artificial insufficiency, and it has made our appetite for utopia dwindle down to almost nothing' (Lewis 86). Conventional personal love is a kind of austerity and also an excuse for austerity, for the state to withhold essential support and transfer collective responsibilities to the family as a unit of supposedly endless generosity.

Lewis looks beyond the nuclear family as a model of political agency, shelter, or microcosm of the state, to seek out historical instances of 'mothering outside of motherhood – and outside even of *womanhood* as it was defined in white supremacist law and science' – as a 'collective art' associated with 'abolitionist

---

[38] Joy James, *In Pursuit of Revolutionary Love: Precarity, Power, Communities* (Brussels: Divided, 2022), xvi.
[39] Jasper Bernes, Joshua Clover, and Juliana Spahr, 'Self-Abolition of the Poet (Part 3)', *Jacket* 2 (2014): http://jacket2.org/commentary/self-abolition-poet-part-3.
[40] Sophie Lewis, *Abolish the Family: A Manifesto for Care and Liberation* (London: Verso, 2022), 2.
[41] Lola Olufemi, *Experiments in Imagining Otherwise* (London: Hajar Press, 2021), 69.

desire and alternative visions of social reproduction'. One example Lewis gives is Alexandra Kollontai's vision of Red Love, 'a social love: a love of many in many ways' (50), in which the family withers away, its functions provided collectively. Another example we could add is Olufemi's desire for love as the

> boundlessness of giving up, giving in, giving over
> to one person, or five people, or 500 people (70)

Not the boundedness of private property, the nuclear family, scarcity, or the poets' love for one another, but a multiplication beyond boundaries, beyond borders, crowding the margin and resisting normal justification.

The poets discussed in this Element are passionate about social love. Femi explores the love of friends in struggles against poverty and the police. Kapil resists the intrusive bodily intimacies pursued by the host nation against an immigrant guest, while staging new expressions of embodied love on borders and in the street. Spahr traces the loves of occupants, both the anti-state and anti-authoritarian Occupy movement, and the settler colonialist, as well as the loves of humans alongside more-than-human others. Boyer takes up the social love that sustains ill and disabled bodies, traduced by capitalism that limits the practices of solidarity and care. Each of these poetries challenges the artificial and repressive versions of subjectivisation possible under capitalism as paltry substitutes for commonality, and envisions ways of being numerous.[42]

Key to each of the projects discussed in this Element is a tenderness towards the multiple, imagined through and against the individuating modes of lyric and its 'unloved' subjects. Femi speaks for and with a group of working-class Black youth whose affiliations in mourning reject the categories of suspicion through which they are seen by the white middle class, and the accusatory, individuating gaze of the police. Kapil allegorises the multiplicity of migration and its complex, traumatic histories as a guest-host dyad, satirising the domesticated couple form and the relationship between love and force in settler colonial regimes. Spahr writes from the perspective of 'they' and 'yous' and 'we', proposing erotic intimacies with worldly structures of domination and resource extraction from a body that respires war and chemical residues. Boyer's communist critique of privatisation, including the privileging of kin-based relationships by the state, is sharpened by the experience of cancer and its treatments, finding solidarity with other suffering bodies and envisioning new architectures and commons where they could meet to offer mutual aid. If poetry's long history records 'the love of many in many ways', these poets diversify and expand their

---

[42] On this topic see also Oren Izenberg, *Being Numerous: Poetry and the Ground of Social Life* (Princeton, NJ: Princeton University Press, 2011).

objects beyond the edgeless grid, towards the revolutionary horizon, and reinvent the lyric along the way. The aim of *Radical Tenderness* is to introduce their work and its political and theoretical contributions to new readers. Mainly, however, I wrote it to honour the possibilities that emerge at that limit: for lyric, and for us.

1 Caleb Femi

Caleb Femi's debut collection from 2020, *Poor*, is described as a monument to 'the North Peckham Estate', 'a troubled yet enchanted world' in south London where Femi grew up. *Poor* explores racialised working-class life on a social housing estate; it's about 'what it feels like to be Black here: like you're dead & alive at the same time'.[43] Fred Moten calls Black performance a 'lyricism of the surplus', and *Poor* exemplifies that lyricism in its 'message of love' to the Black urban working class, a surplus population and thriving community Femi calls 'Mandem': 'I wouldn't refer to middle class black people as Mandem. So it's very class specific as well as race specific.'[44] But the book also turns to the 'outer world', asking 'What is your perception of working-class "poor" people – and poor Black people specifically? What do you know about us and how has that shaped your understanding of the trials and tribulations that we face?'[45] These questions are posed in *Poor*, where a literal gatekeeper addresses the intrusive reader: 'What do you know about this story – the full of it?' (5). *Poor* is full of such shibboleths, resisting the intrusions of middle-class readers through a defence of its subjects' opacity. At the same time, the book explores Peckham's concrete exteriors and softened interiors, depicting its vulnerable subjects as a collective who emerge into lyric individualism in moments of danger.

Femi has said, 'I wanted to police the imaginations of people who, when they think about the community the book is about, think of mug shots or violent images or reductive in their preoccupation.' He critiques the way such readers 'become voyeurs of the whole experience', sympathising but 'with a God complex that does nothing but reinforce their position in everything'. The challenge, then, is not to appeal for sympathy to what Gillian Rose calls the 'ultimate predator', the reader who can identify with any victim in a narrative of

---

[43] Caleb Femi, *Poor* (London: Penguin, 2020), 31.

[44] Fred Moten, *In the Break: The Aesthetics of the Black Radical Tradition* (Minneapolis, MN: University of Minnesota Press, 2003), 26. Bridget Minamore, 'Get Up, Stand Up Now: Q&A with Poet and Director Caleb Femi', *Somerset House* blog (28 August 2019), www.somerset house.org.uk/blog/get-stand-now-qa-poet-and-director-caleb-femi.

[45] 'Caleb Femi and Athian Akec in Conversation', *Huck* (21 December 2020), www.huckmag .com/art-and-culture/caleb-femi-and-athian-akec-in-conversation/.

cruelty, but who rarely imagines themselves in the role of persecutor.[46] If 'the police don't listen. They're not here. They're not actually present', nor does the privileged reader listen, or be present, to the lives honoured in his book.[47] Instead of courting this absent reader, Femi's work celebrates experiences of kinship and community whose linguistic matter resists seizure by outsiders, addressing his community as an intimate public. Simultaneously Femi works to divest middle-class readers of their voyeurism and power: poetry may be 'owned' by the middle class, but he is writing for and about working-class people.[48] These aims give the lie to Femi's claim that he is 'not a political poet'. Femi's poetry enacts a deeply political critique of capital, racialisation, and poverty through the specificities of lived experience.

This section argues that Femi challenges the individuation of feeling within the private spaces where lyric traditionally dwells. *Poor*'s subjects are rarely solitary; the lyric 'I' emerges mostly in encounters with trauma or the police. They thrive and struggle together, as a collective whose sociality is the source of the book's power and pleasure. *Poor* constructs a compensatory architecture for its residents, one in which their struggles are resolutely communal, even as they are interpreted through – and sometimes even become – the hardness of the blocks they inhabit. I focus here on the role of the built environment in Femi's poetics of the Black working class, and the way he celebrates and grieves the tenderness of the collective in their struggles not to resemble the concrete world – both the buildings of North Peckham, and an impoverished materiality, unable to rise to the abstraction of spirit except in death. *Poor* also grapples with the paradox of aestheticisation: that the loving witness of the poem might not do more than decorate the brutalism of that architecture, under the watchful eye of the middle-class reader. Alongside their celebrations of community and creativity, Femi's poems seek a different form of shelter for the opacity of his subjects, one that necessitates a new approach to lyric individualism.

Resisting Individuality

Poor is a work of mourning. Its chronology extends from the murder of the ten-year-old Black child Damilola Taylor in North Peckham in 2000, to the

---

[46] Gillian Rose, *Mourning Becomes the Law: Philosophy and Representation* (Cambridge: Cambridge University Press, 1996), 47.

[47] Ciaran Thapar, 'Caleb Femi's Poetry Shatters Stereotypes around Black British Youth', *i-D* (25 January 2021), https://i-d.vice.com/en_uk/article/bvxp3m/interview-with-poet-and-artist-caleb-femi-poor.

[48] Robert Kazandjian, '"In Any Circumstance, Humans Need Imagination in Order to Survive": An Interview with Caleb Femi', *Complex* (19 November 2020): www.complex.com/pop-culture/2020/11/caleb-femi-interview.

corporate and political murder of seventy-two working-class people by fire in Grenfell Tower in North Kensington in 2017. The book's wake work includes rituals of commemoration that respond to racism, defined in Ruth Wilson Gilmore's terms as 'the state-sanctioned or extralegal production and exploitation of group-differentiated vulnerability to premature death'.[49] Among those rituals are the 2011 riots following the murder of Mark Duggan by police in Tottenham, which Femi says was a way that Black and working-class people 'demanded payment for death' (*Poor* 30). In Femi's account, journalists misinterpret the speech and speech acts of the rioters: the media hears 'demanded', when the rioters say '*de / man / dead*'. The connection between death and demand links Duggan's death, through the echo of the title of Wole Soyinka's prison notebook *The Man Died*, to an internationalist resistance to anti-Black and colonial violence. The action painting of the rioters, who smashed sites of commerce and alienation and burned police cars across the United Kingdom, is allied with localised scenes of grief, family funerals, private libations, and community memorials. Set within this political frame of anti-Black violence, riot, and resistance, *Poor* uses familiar lyric devices such as natural metaphor to convey the vulnerability of its subjects. But it works hard to honour the people, languages, imaginations, and realities of the estate without exposing them to a voyeuristic or policing gaze.

A great deal has been written about the historical struggle of Black authors, as Erica Hunt says, 'to invent the person for whom poetry is possible'.[50] Femi's aim is not to concede to white supremacist or classist power that wants only to 'sip on the ripe mourning of the poor' (114) and eavesdrop on trauma 'like pub chatter' (115). He constantly weighs up the urge to 'humanise' his subjects as individuals: to prove to white readers that 'my poor people, my browner people, my *other* people who are not seen as people' (116) are in fact people *just like us*, with recognisable aspirations and fears, and so on. His book tries not to dwell on universal equivalences that might elicit feelings of sympathy for poor boys, feelings that middlebrow readers of poetry can safely take comfort in. Instead, to document the interior lives of the 'youts robbed of youth', whose stories are told in the records of contemporary media only as tragedy or threat, Femi resists particularising his subjects. *Poor* doesn't represent the boys' unique individuality as a token of their right to enter the class of bourgeois subjects who – in Hegel's terms – are able to 'stamp' the object world with their 'inner consciousness' and raise their 'inner life' and singularity to 'a universal validity' in lyric

---

[49] Ruth Wilson Gilmore, *Golden Gulag: Prisons, Surplus, Crisis, and Opposition in Globalizing California* (Berkeley, CA: University of California Press, 2007), 28.

[50] Erica Hunt, 'Response to Race and the Poetic Avant-Garde', *Boston Review* (10 March 2015), http://bostonreview.net/.

form.[51] The individual in *Poor* is not 'torn free from the collective' and able to 'flash out' in his struggle against the topic; he is determined by the collective, including by the way that collective is perceived by the class of people who read Penguin books of poetry and award the Forward Prize. But the collective – mandem, community, kinship – offers sustenance, pleasure, safety, and tenderness.

Living in a country where the white imaginary reduces young Black working-class subjects to a punitive sameness, Femi's poems seek out the political power in that interchangeability. In 'Schrödinger's Black', for example, he recognises a photo of Mark Duggan. 'It was a picture of me even though I wasn't dead' (30), the speaker affirms, before transforming the commonality of racialised suffering into the shared action of riot: 'I wasn't there, but I thought I was – my brazen face live on the nation's screens.' Femi's poems work through and against this fungibility of the Black subject. 'Thirteen' recollects being stopped and searched by the same officer who had visited the speaker's primary school. The speaker hopes to be seen as a smiling, tender boy, not the 'description of a man' for which he has been taken (16). Singled out and adultified, 'you' cannot convey your worth and specificity to feds in search of a type – 'you fit / the description', and so the encounter follows its conventional script. In the white/policing gaze, any Black person is indistinguishable from others.

The temptation might be to use lyric's subjectivising powers to enrich these punitive categories with more valorised, individuated selves. But the poems do something different, offering a resistant form of interchangeability through repeated episodes of exchange. In 'Concrete (I)', the speaker bequeaths his 'only pair of Air Max 90s' to an intimately addressed 'you', so that the trainers might 'lift you up seven feet tall', and you can walk 'proud, / for you walk in what I might have been' (19). If Black youth is picked out in the policing gaze by its appearance, particularly its fashions, 'outfits cold like a Gucci Mane ad-lib' (28) and coveted trainers, Femi uses the commodity as a marker of continuity between fellows: the shoes create a link between 'I' as impoverished benefactor (who has nothing else to give but the object and the wish for thriving that they represent), and 'you' the heir (empowering the next generation while also casting over it a shadow of untimely death). In 'Barter', the poem that opens the book, a different exchange takes place: the speaker wants to trade with a more privileged 'you'. He trades faces, 'your benefit of the doubt' for 'my doubt of innocence', 'my' kin 'scattered like dust mite in the wind' for 'your pristine family tree', 'my' voice box 'for when you need to rap hiphop songs' (3). Unlike

---

[51] Hegel, *Aesthetics*, 2:1111.

the bequeathing of an inheritance, using the commodity as a memorial of relatedness, in this poem it is the lyric 'I' itself that is an object of exchange. The speaker's body and fortune can be stripped for parts and monetised by the privileged other who enjoys 'a holiday home in Costa Blanca' (notably, the white coast) while 'I' labour in Peckham.

'Barter' sits at the front of the collection as a warning about appropriation and how the value generated by Black artists is accumulated by white institutions that own the means of production, including the production of literary prestige. It is accompanied by an image that I will discuss later, of a person hidden inside a large, inscrutable hoodie. Rinaldo Walcott suggests that a way of reading oversize clothing styles on Black men

> is to account for what cannot be seen or visualised by the clothing – a body made useless ... A *saggin' pants ethics* ... requires us to grapple with the ways that Black poor people's creative energies resist being hijacked by capitalisation and resist forms of financialisation by engaging a practice of uselessness that cannot be cannibalised by capital but nonetheless references Black life as a life worth living in the face of a global system that seeks only to use and/or discard the Black life-form.[52]

Femi – despite his resistance to middle-class voyeurism – has been taken up by the culture industry, with profiles in *i-D* and *Elle Decoration*, and a film made in collaboration with upscale clothing retailer Whistles. At issue is not how Femi chooses to monetise his image (he has spoken candidly about the struggles to survive as an artist without family wealth), but how these firms hijack poor Black people's creative energies, appropriating their cultural and aesthetic production to extract value from the endz. As Femi himself inadvertently admits, the imagination 'is one of our most valuable commodities in the struggle for liberation, equality and humanisation of Black people'.[53] His poems reflect the difficulty of this position, as the speaker transitions away from the estate, becoming part of the gentrified 'good part' of Hackney (122), landing on 'the other side of the street', which means 'the hood won't take me back' (121) – a fear of the loss of community that goes along with certain forms of class mobility, and is a consequence of his successful self-fashioning as a lyric poet.

But what is most striking about Femi's representation of North Peckham is the consistency with which it provides a lyric collectivisation of subjectivity. These are poems about 'residents on the brink' (14) and 'Boys who live by the

---

[52] Rinaldo Walcott, *The Long Emancipation: Moving toward Black Freedom* (Durham, NC: Duke University Press, 2021), 88, 90.

[53] Femi and Akec in conversation, *Huck*.

code / & stay sealed up with wax' (11), about 'all the girls' who 'call us trouble' (12), 'Dark skin boys', 'boys who play out here' (21), 'hooded boys with overgrown nails' (30), 'us poor kids from the block' (39), 'trap legends' (47), '*youngers* sprawled like a deck of trick cards' and 'little cousins' (50), a congregation in which 'you sit in rows with the other boys' (58), 'four boys in a Honda' (63), '20 closed-petal boys uniformed' (65), the 'Shirland Massive' – 'children / labelled *thugs & crooked*' who are 'theatrical in their play' (86), boys who are perceived as interchangeable by the police, misidentified, harassed, stopped, and searched, 'Peckham Boys', boys happy to be together, not differentiated individuals, rarely solitary lyric 'I's.

In *Poor*, the individual is not the consummation of lyric privacy and legal rights, but an isolated figure who tends to emerge in violent encounters with whiteness, the state, and the police. Its 'I' is troubled; singleness makes 'me' vulnerable. In 'Mandem', the speaker looks from one side of the block at another group, wondering 'what will they think of me if I approach with my / own body clutched between my hands' (67). 'They', the collective, are an impressive 'peacock' assemblage of reckless gamblers, 'entangled roses' whose laughter emits sparks. The speaker desires belonging but hesitates at the threshold where he is still an unguarded individual. Even the joyful 'Here Too Spring Comes to Us with Open Arms' ends by imagining a lone boy who 'walks through the park / no police no *opps* only the company of spirits' (51). The boy is protected and nourished by ethereal companions; but threat lingers in this fantasy of exceptional solitude.

The singular 'I' tends to emerge in this collection under the force of the police gaze, or in the solitude of the cell or hospital ward. 'Two Bodies Caught in One Cell' imagines a boy praying in a South London police cell, attended by a 'sibling' who keeps his dangerous company (the poem invokes Cain and Abel) but also watches over him as the figure of sleep. The image of imaginary companionship is a spell to counteract the intolerable reality of a boy, alone, in the cell's darkness; but it merely underlines the desperate loneliness of the incarcerated child. The individual emerges most consistently in the sixth section of the book, which documents the traumatic experiences suffered by the speaker. Femi himself was shot in the leg at age seventeen. In 'Repress', the speaker has suffered a gunshot wound and is lying in a hospital bed, interrogated by police while death 'drifted / through the ward like a gardener' (97). The repressed memory of the shooting is displaced by poetic details without forensic utility: 'I saw milk / dripping / from the udder of a car . . . / the sky a locked gate', and so on (97). The boy writing the poem resists the police and the reader's need for information, the moment of his wounding hidden behind a poetic invention that offers limited relief.

'Survivor's Guilt' itemises other traumatic experiences: 'Run over, twice. / Stabbed. / Shot. / A car crash'. Guilt and PTSD make him lonely, separating him from the community's rituals of mutual care, until 'my presence at funerals felt like bragging' (32). The speaker's unlikely survival isolates him from the community of the grieving and the dead. While he confesses 'that I want to live for good times', 'every day, on the endz, there is a procession / my breathing body mocks' (33). The neighbourhood (endz) and the poem's ends conflict with the breath that continually flows through the speaker's warm, individuated body. For 'the boy writing this poem', it feels *'like death is a party / all his friends were invited to but him'* (72). When the self loses its sheltering typicality within the collective through death, injury, or vulnerability, or suffers the cursed singularity of the survivor, it is also haunted by the spectres of all who have been lost:

> I am a museum of all
> the ghosts I could have been.
> Why me – when better boys
> deserved life (32)

Those boys include 'Edvin', who 'took a blade to the gut' and so is distinguished by name from 'we who did not know how to weep' ('Concrete (III)', 69). Death individuates; grief is shared collectively. As Femi says in an interview, 'I don't ever want to forget the truth of the fact that I'm not special. None of us are special because of where we are right now. And when I say that, we're not more special than the people who didn't make it. ... We were fortunate enough to end up on a different side of the consequence.'[54] While the living 'we' are 'not special', *Poor* catalogues rituals of memorialisation and sociality as ways of holding onto the particularity of the dead. These rituals animate a particular place, North Peckham, as both a necropolis and site of Black working-class joy. But the estate is a complex symbol in this book. Femi analyses the relationship between its history and class and racialised struggle in the UK through the medium of concrete, while also depicting retreats into softened interiors as spaces of sheltering communality, joy, and sorrow.

Defensible Space: Architecture and Authority in North Peckham

In *Poor*, North Peckham is represented as in part a place of constant struggle, of anti-Black violence, police harassment, poverty, hunger, and oppression. Femi specifies that the book's preoccupation is not 'violence done by people within the community' but 'structural violence. State-sanctioned violence.

---

[54] Kazandjian, 'In Any Circumstance'.

The violence that is enacted on the people. The letting down of safety regulations of their houses. Dilapidated conditions people live in. Lack of infrastructure, lack of opportunities'.[55] This structural violence is active not only in policing, schooling, and other interactions with state power, but in the built environment itself:

> we watched a Vietnam war film
> & saw a regular Tuesday
> just more confetti
> & though their trenches weren't
> suspended corridors like ours
> the gist was the same (75)

The poem's unpunctuated rhythms and duplicated ampersands reduce its comparisons to a weary 'gist', an easily captured parallel: that people of colour in the 'first world' of South London endure imperialist violence that aligns them with the Global South (Peckham is pronounced '*pek narm*', according to the poem), even if the spatiality of these encounters is different (trenches versus suspended corridors). That alignment was central to Black and anti-colonial organising in the 1970s, but in Femi's example it is reduced to commodified representation, a reductive bottom line that suggests capitulation: 'just more confetti' exploding its papery ordinance over the militarised streets.

The alignment between South London and the Global South also reflects the circulation of people and resources between colonised countries and the metropole. Femi was born in Nigeria in 1990 and moved to London at the age of seven. Despite the violence which is a constant presence in the book, 'I have never loved anything the way I love the endz' (129). Femi recalls of his childhood that 'the threat of violence was normalised'. But what replaces lost innocence 'is a tenacity to thrive, to want to have a good time in spite of whatever conditions you live in. It made me want to have more fun in life and embrace joy'.[56] The book documents a shared practice of thriving through intimacy, sociality, and pleasure, in which residents transform the estate through the power of their imaginations. In Peckham, young people 'are joyous and full of imagination. They embrace fantasy'. One morning a miraculous new mural appears on the wall, which 'birthed so much beautiful folklore: there were stories of people running through walls, or turning into cats – because of that painting'. On Mondays, the stairwells were washed in detergent that smelled of bubblegum, and suddenly become 'a wonderland where everything felt shiny

---

[55] Thapar, 'Caleb Femi's Poetry'.

[56] Ellen Peirson-Hagger, 'Caleb Femi: "Poetry Is the Art of the People"', *New Statesman* (28 October 2020): www.newstatesman.com/culture/observations/2020/10/caleb-femi-north-peckham-estate-police-poetry-teaching.

and bouncy'.[57] Femi's poems attend to the myths and folklore of the estate, the oral histories and visual records of a resolute magic that infuses it. In this way, Femi aims to capture the '"in-spiteness" of working-class people, how they exist in spite of everything that is structurally working against them, everything that is reducing their standard of living and trying to compromise their quality of life'.[58]

Poems are in-spite places, sites of imaginary habitation, whose analogy with living space is apparent in the word 'stanza': the pretty rooms of the sonnet are constructed by formal arrangements on the page and the architecture of repeating elements such as rhyme, to draw permeable boundaries between outward and inward experience. Within the architectural enclosure of the poem, a lifeworld can be wilfully arranged, a space of scarcity or abundance, constraint or freedom, deprivation or empowerment. Femi's work does this, while also unpicking the structural intimacies of the lyric poem, opening its scene onto a housing estate where public and private, domestic and civic relations become ambivalent. Before discussing his depictions of intimate interiors in North Peckham, I'll offer a brief history of the estate and its representation in *Poor*.

The North Peckham estate was a low-density response to the failed high-rise constructions of the 1950s. Consisting of over 1400 homes in sixty-five five-storey blocks, it was built across a forty-acre site in 1966. The architects sought to realise the 'streets in the sky' model pioneered by Le Corbusier. Homes were connected by walkways, where residents and visitors could pass between shops and amenities and avoid 'the dirt, noise and danger of London traffic'.[59] In this urban pastoral, communities could congregate and children play in safety, held above the chaos of the city; 'The housewife can open the door to the tradesman much as she does in an ordinary street. The children can also run around unmolested by traffic, just as they used to do in the days of hopscotch and the hoop.'[60] It is a vision of intergenerational family life that privileges children's safety, health and play, a return to old-fashioned values within a Modernist vision.

But in Femi's view, the architects 'created a design that allowed for a self-governing community: outreach, and the relationship with the police and other

---

[57] Claire Armitstead, 'Caleb Femi: "Henceforth I'm Solely Preoccupied with Being a Merchant of Joy"', *Guardian* (30 October 2020), www.theguardian.com/books/2020/oct/30/caleb-femi-henceforth-im-solely-preoccupied-with-being-a-merchant-of-joy. This memory is reflected in 'Because of the Times' (13).

[58] 'Caleb Femi: "I See Myself as an Archivist"', *Penguin* blog (6 November 2020): www.penguin.co.uk/articles/2020/november/caleb-femi-poor-interview.html.

[59] 'Life at Deck Level', *Southwark Civic News* (July 1968); cited in John Boughton, *Municipal Dreams: The Rise and Fall of Council Housing* (London: Verso, 2018), 179–184.

[60] H. F. Wallis, 'A Living Showpiece at North Peckham?', *Municipal Review* (November 1972), cited in John Boughton, *A History of Council Housing in 100 Estates* (London: RIBA, 2022), chap. 7.

services, was a poor one'.[61] Self-governance does not mean community autonomy. Instead, the architecture felt like a punitive enclosure.

> When a space is designed that way, what you're doing is keeping people in
> a mini prison, ostracising them physically and telling them they're not part of
> the city, that they are physically othered. When everything around you is
> bricks and concrete, it limits your quality of life … The state of the space in
> which you live tells you how much you're worth.[62]

The middle-class, individualist modern architect might wish to absent himself
from the city as a site of danger and pollution, but his brutalist model suspends
residents from full participation while also preventing them from accessing
anything 'natural'. Residents internalise the estate's veneration of concrete and
shoddy structures as expressions of their own value to capital.

Poor is in dialogue with the history of social housing in the UK and the
ideologies that shaped that history. In her 1985 book *Utopia on Trial*, Alice
Coleman criticised projects like North Peckham as part of a programme of
'paternalistic authority' that trapped people in unchosen environments.[63] Coleman
produced a 'disadvantagement score' for each building as the basis for a proposed
programme of renovation of the UK's social housing stock. Her writing drew on
carceral logics, her moral emphasis falling always on the degenerative influence of
these buildings on children.[64] With her view of the city space as a war of all against
all, Coleman's work was informed by Oscar Newman's notion of 'defensible
space' – a violent theory of social control based on individual territorialism.[65]
Newman correlated building height to recorded crime and attributed the safety of
low-rise dwellings to a sense of communal ownership of spaces beyond the front
door. He proposed a system of barriers and surveillance to assert control over
disputed social space and to overcome the 'fear' that 'eats away' at those condemned to live in social housing. Newman glorified policing and
securitisation, and his work is an astonishing enactment of whiteness as property.[66]

Both Newman and Coleman blamed the decline of social housing on design
flaws, rather than managed neglect motivated by class and racial prejudice.
Utopia on Trial was read by Margaret Thatcher, who recognised its affinity with
her own neoliberal assault on communities. Coleman met with Thatcher at
Downing Street in 1988 and explained that problems of anti-social behaviour

---

[61] Peirson-Hagger, 'Caleb Femi'. [62] Kazandjian, 'In Any Circumstance'.

[63] Alice Coleman, *Utopia on Trial: Vision and Reality in Planned Housing* (London: Hilary Shipman, 1985), 6.

[64] Alice Coleman, 'The Psychology of Housing', *The Salisbury Review* (Winter 2009): 10–12 (10).

[65] Oscar Newman, *Defensible Space: People and Design in the Violent City* (London: Architectural Press, 1972).

[66] Cheryl Harris, 'Whiteness as Property', *Harvard Law Review* 106.8 (June 1993): 1707–1791.

and violence 'occurred far more frequently in tall blocks of flats than in traditional houses'.[67] Coleman persuaded Thatcher to create a £50 million fund to allow her 'to redesign seven misery estates' in different parts of the country.[68] Despite significant criticisms of her work, Coleman's advice led to the demolition of North Peckham's walkways and creation of front and rear gardens (or 'defensible space') by the new ground floor entrances to the flats.[69] Coleman later criticised Southwark council's efforts to improve the estate, even claiming 'that if I had been allowed to make the North Peckham Estate as safe as the areas I improved elsewhere, the Damiola Taylor [*sic*] tragedy would have been most unlikely'.[70]

As the ideological arrogance of Newman and Coleman's work demonstrates, the housing estate has long been a site of intense conflict between the state (both the central British government and local, often more progressive, councils) and the needs of exploited surplus populations. In the 1980s, council budgets were slashed. Under the 1980 Housing Act, which gave council tenants the right to buy their homes, social housing stock diminished and housing shortages became acute. Dispossession severed communal bonds and sent the estate into a cascade of decline. Many empty units became what Femi refers to as 'trap houses' (squatted for drug sales and use) and 'bandos' or abandoned dwellings.[71] The scarcity of public housing, which simultaneously generated massive wealth for London's propertied class, meant that the remaining units were desperately overcrowded: 'Your flat was in the north: / one bedroom and seven bodies making do' (*Poor* 13). Femi's generation grew up amidst constant construction and threats to demolish their homes. By the early 2000s, most of the North Peckham estate had been 'transformed from pits of urban blight into shining examples of regeneration', one journalist wrote[72] – a transformation by capital from social-democratic provision of community housing for all, to private ownership and discriminatory social mobility created by London's enormous housing bubble. As Femi observes, suddenly Peckham is on the list

---

[67] P. A. Bearpark, Private Secretary to Margaret Thatcher, letter (19 January 1988), Prime Ministerial Private Office files (PREM19/2240): https://331215bb933457d2988b-6db7349bced3 b64202e14ff100a12173.ssl.cf1.rackcdn.com/PREM19/1990/PREM19-2240.pdf.

[68] Coleman, 'Psychology of Housing', 10.

[69] Graham Towers, *Shelter Is Not Enough: Transforming Multi-storey Housing* (London: Policy Press, 2000), 115.

[70] Alice Coleman, 'Design Disadvantage in Southwark', *The Dulwich Society Journal* (Summer 2008).

[71] Information in the preceding two paragraphs is from John Boughton's *Municipal Dreams* blog, which Femi quotes in 'Because of the Times': 'The Five Estates, Peckham', https://municipal dreams.wordpress.com/2016/10/25/the-five-estates-peckham-part-iii/.

[72] Vikki Miller, 'Peckham Rise', *Building* (8 October 2004): www.building.co.uk/peckham-rise/ 3041666.article.

of *Time Out*'s 'Best New Places to Live' (38), a transition watched by a wary community: '*When hipsters take selfies / on the corners where our / friends died, the rent goes up*' (39). Peckham's gentrification, like that of another historically Black neighbourhood nearby in Brixton, has led to the displacement of tenants and community hubs by shiny new developments and hipster restaurants. 'Because of the Times' reflects on this history, asking:

> Is this what the architect had in mind?
> A paradise of affordable bricks, tucked under
> a blanket, shielded from the world –
> all that hopeful good on powder-blue paper,
> measured lines defining angles
> of respite for the poor (13)

The poem records the difference between the architect's utopian vision and the estate's materiality; and yet the poem is also a thing 'in mind', written in 'measured lines' on paper, powder-blue or otherwise, seeking to offer its own 'respite for the poor'. This book of selves is arguably part of the cultural transformation of Peckham that brings the hipsters and their selfies.

But Femi suggests that within this paradise, a malevolent force was already at work: while 'nothing the estate raised was a monster, yet / the devil found good ground to plough his seeds'. The vision is moralising in ways that recall Coleman's critique of 'misery estates' in *Utopia on Trial*. The poem ends with Taylor's murder, one of the most publicly grieved deaths of Black children in London in recent decades, and another instance in which the single individual is made vulnerable:

> It is true on paper there were no designs for a tomb
> yet the East wing stairs were where Damilola was found:
> blue dawn, blue body, blue lights, blue tapes. (14)

Referring to the blue used throughout the North Peckham design, the blue corpse emptied of blood and oxygen, and the blue police light and tape, the poem's parallel structure traces a rhetorical, visual, and real symmetry between architecture, violence, and the police. In some ways, the poem echoes Coleman's determinism and her claim that fixing design flaws could have prevented Taylor's death. Femi exposes the limits of social planning: the buildings offered no blanket, shield, or respite to a boy dying alone in a public stairwell. A little boy's living warmth disperses across the corridors, his red blood gone blue.

The Concrete Body

Bhanu Kapil writes in her book *Ban en Banlieue* about the history of earlier race riots in London – specifically the confrontation with the National Front in

Southall in 1979 that led to the death of Blair Peach. Her book imagines the way riots 'overlay' one another: 'The riot is a charnel ground in this sense – overlain – in the present – by concrete – poured right down – over the particular spot on the sidewalk I am speaking of – as well as – migrations.'[73] I will return to this work in Section 2. This imagined riot shares a lineage with Femi's depiction of concrete as a resistant form that residents must inhabit, imbue with life and feeling, and/or overturn in order to access a softened shelter in which they are safe enough to become individuated. Like Kapil, Femi also sees concrete as a burial site and place of ritual libation.

In 'Coping' – a term that is both emotional and architectural (for the top course of a wall) – Femi ties architecture to mourning. Here, the collective 'dark skin boys' are scared of the dark, poised 'on a ledge' (21) mimicked by line endings. The poem's tercets act as miniature gatherings where they shout across dark spaces: '*Are you safe, my g?*'. The poem personifies the estate as an entombed body:

> maybe an estate, tall as it is,
> is the half-buried femur of a dead god,
> and the blue light of dawn
>
> – his son in mourning –
> looks on the things we do
> when there is one less boy among us.
>
> How we pour the holy spirit out of the bottle
> onto the concrete where his ashes lie,
> stir it into a clay, mould it into a new body
>
> and like a kite in fading wind
> watch his soul sink back to good earth,
> settle into his body like he never left. (21)

Taylor died while living in a building that was gradually being 'decanted' – emptied in preparation for its demolition.[74] The liquidation of the residents is reframed in this poem, in which a memorial libation infuses the boy bodily and

---

[73] Bhanu Kapil, *Ban en Banlieu* (New York, NY: Nightboat, 2015), 21.

[74] A resident, 'Steve', explained that Damilola lived in a building 'on its way to being decanted, you know, that's the expression that used to be used . . . they'd empty people from the blocks . . . before the block went to be demolished, and . . . he was living in a half maintained block, and he . . . it was an area that at that time somehow they weren't . . . the electrics, the lights were going out, and they were getting water, and there were squatters . . . and it was . . . it all added to a feeling of . . . complete decay, when in fact, that was one of the last bits that was actually gonna be changed, but you know people . . . "oh the North Peckham Estate, how horrendous it is" but actually it was . . . it was being in the process of being renewed.' Luna Glucksberg, *Wasting the Inner-City: Waste, Value and Anthropology on the Estates*. PhD diss., Goldsmiths, University of London (2013), 116: https://research.gold.ac.uk/id/eprint/8715/.

spiritually into the clay and concrete of the estate. The ritual allows participants to cycle through birth, death, and rebirth, within and as the heaviness of the estate. 'Coping' acknowledges 'the things we do when one of us is either seriously injured or killed, the ritualistic coping mechanisms that fortify our sense of community, that sort of make us feel that we are able to rely on each other. And in some weird way make us able to be emotional in a space that is often devoid of emotion'.[75] Lyric poems and mourning rituals are both kinds of performance that modulate the brutal objectivity of architecture and force it to bear the imprint of its inhabitants' grief.

Across the book, the estate is a decayed body, a skeleton impervious to attack, devoid of emotion. Femi's personification of the estate as body echoes tropes of the diseased body politic and of twentieth-century utopian architecture, and particularly Le Corbusier's *Ville Radieuse* (Radiant City), whose form was modelled on the human body. In 'Cold', 'its spine already pokes from concrete' (28). In 'Because Of the Times', it is 'a system of nerves' (13). But the body also become part of the estate. In 'Yard', Femi maps the bodily interior as a series of bracketed houses, including the house that is a home (and so determined by an emotional relation), the house that is rented or squatted (and so determined by an exchange relation), and the house that is the site of power (determined less by a political relation of enfranchisement than by the monopoly of violence):

> all the [houses]
> I have lived in sit in my ribcage
> with faces like beggars . . .
> I take myself on a tour through my self
> each circle of [house] is visited
> you see this [house] here under my left lung . . .
> I could not feed anyone a supper but I
> kept love in this [house] . . . (109)

The architectural brackets enclose the word 'house', building a secure site that is also blocked off from the rest of the sentence. They slow the poem down, forcing a pause to contemplate what else might be inserted within them, as alternative meanings and realities offer themselves as possible completions of the poem's inventory. Just as *Poor* takes the outsider reader on a deliberately evasive tour of the estate, this poem offers a parodic tour of the self, hiding identifying details behind a generic marker of place. As the poem reflects the capacity of the residents to exceed their architectural constraints, it breaks out of these brackets and spills over the line break:

> I kept a shoobs invited the whole endz to this
> cramped corner of the world we grew enormous
> yak spilled on skirts air ached with sweet sweat
> daggering gyal zoot ashed on my windowsill
> I held a shoobs every night they swaggered
> back like the legs of tarantulas swimming through
> the dark we supped on this only (109)

This enjambed, abundant passage is an example of the book's 'message of love' to the Black working class. Using diction that sends a middle-class reader like me to the Urban Dictionary, the poem shows how a 'cramped corner of the world' can grow past the constraints of the line ending, the building, or poverty into a celebration of social life: girls, cognac, sweat, smoke crammed into a space of plentifulness. But the party depicted here is also an echo of the tragic one hosted for Yvonne Ruddock and Angela Jackson's birthdays in New Cross in 1981, in which thirteen young people were killed by a fire that many suspected was the result of an arson attack by white supremacists:

> between songs we christened this [house]
> NEW BLACK [HOUSE] OR [HOUSE] OF COMMONS
> kept eight buckets of water in the [house]'s eight corners
> because there were enough of us in there to die by fire (109–10)

The house is Black because it's racialised, but also because it's burnt. It is a space for nourishment and sociality that is constantly under threat. The House of Commons is a parody of the commons that this poem, all these poems, long for. But the singers can also imagine burning that House down and building a New Black House to take its place.

Throughout *Poor*, the speaker inhabits an architecture whose flaws are material projections of the racist state and racialised capitalism. But the poems also disclose a process of introjection in which architecture becomes a set of persecutory internal objects for residents of the estate. Concrete serves as a topos for the built environment and the built persona of the speaker. It is a substance that displaces the natural world. 'Concrete smells like a siege' (8); 'concrete makes me feel safe ... when I leave my block I don't feel safe' (9). Concrete is an impermeable defence against the elements and other people, creating spaces to shelter from harm, while also being a brutal material that blocks feeling and growth. It can be a weapon – blocks pulled up to hurl at the police – and a stage under which, with the Situationists, we can find the beach (or as Femi puts it, 'Beneath the pavement there are rivers of Living Water', 68). It is the anti-abstraction, whose properties include 'courageousness', 'ability to maintain tensile strength even under the weight of a procession, soundlessness when struck (as paving stone) by the fist of the wailing mother, electrical conductivity, propensity to terraform when in contact with a boy's imagination, shrinkage, creep' (68). It is sometimes 'the lining of the womb / that holds boys with their mothers', becoming 'soft as a meadow might a lamb' (69). It supports, it absorbs pain and blood and libations; in one moment of intense emotional exposure, 'I was the marrow of concrete, / making my pain there against its texture' (104). Living in and as concrete has bred the speaker to indifference: 'concrete has made an equilibrium of me. / I am no more a good insulator – I don't hold on' to hate, love, 'or my own chest', and now 'the cold wind will pass through me', tuning me with its 'sugared song' (104). This outer world made of concrete requires people to behave as if they are made of concrete. *Poor* seeks to transform this resistant substance through metaphor, to 'terraform' it through imagination. But sometimes the only thing left to do is to retreat from its brutal reality into the safety of the interior.

Interior Life

In the Introduction, I discussed the idea that lyric was characterised by an 'inward turn', turning its back on public life and the marketplace, turning towards a sacred privacy that is the guarantor of authenticity while also presupposing bourgeois conditions of production for poetry, the individual, and the family. But I also noted that withdrawal into inwardness was a differential process, not equally accessible to all poetic subjects. This is evident in *Poor*, which repeatedly attempts to turn away from the concrete exterior towards interiors as places of safety and abundance. This movement can be seen in 'Gentle Youth', which turns away from the street as a site of political action, towards private spaces of tenderness. The poem begins by foreswearing 'retribution' for suffering: if that is what 'the youts wanted / not one brick would remain on the city's skyline' (27). Femi warns that class conflict is not on the cards: 'We are over such theatrics – for now.' He suggests the riots of 2011 were a failure; instead of coalescing into a revolutionary moment, 'the youts ran in all directions / like scared cattle' (27). But the defensive posturing gives away Femi's understanding of who the poem's readers really are: middle-class readers fearing that 'youts will come / for you in the small of the night', and who need to learn that the boys they fear actually spend the small of the night sleeping like flowers and pigeons, or revelling with their mates. Then, the poem suddenly changes tack. Instead of riotous and dangerous youth, the reader is presented with 'gentle', tender youth engaged in a collective act of listening:

> One of us saw visions of a new home:
> *New world, new sky that's so blue it's black too. – Frank Ocean*
> We are all sat listening to him in tears,
> youts robbed of youth, robbed of a rocking cradle,
> singing the ballad of the youthful:
> *If sorrow must come for us / Let it collect us at our homes.* (27)

With its collage of voices marked by italics and the slash of a lineated quotation, the lyric stages the performance of a lyric. The scene is set for the composition of a new folk ballad. The 'one of us' picked out for his visionary capacity shares it with the others, who respond with tears and dream together of new worlds, new skies. The youths articulate a common hope through song: that sorrow and death will find them at home, in the spaces where they are loved, not alone in the blue dawn of the blue body, blue lights, blue tapes, but beneath a sky so blue it could be black. These Black boys who never got to be children can sing childhood's songs through the medium of this tender lyric. They sing it for themselves first, but they also now sing it for us.

For these boys, as Gwendolyn Brooks may have said, 'Every time I walk out of my house, it is a political decision.'[76] The tension between a concrete external world that requires vigilance, and the various internal worlds in which the self can be safely exposed, is apparent in the photographs that appear in *Poor*. A number of these are of exteriors, highlighting the uniformity of blocks within blocks, each containing separate lives; or of securitised public spaces with police milling around the entrances. Others are of people, including some of Femi's own childhood. The images represent the antithetical conditions of Black life on the estate: on the one hand, raciality enforced by state violence, iconic Black death made for consumption by outsiders, the publicisation of the Black body in civic space; on the other, the tenderness of individuals, children, at home, consenting to make themselves available to the intimacy of the camera, pictured in states of relaxation, celebration, and relation.

Writing about the terrible photograph of the body of Michael Brown left exposed in the street, Fred Moten and Stefano Harney imagine another image:

> If we refuse to show the image of a lonely body, of the outline of the space that body simultaneously took and left, we do so in order to imagine jurisgenerative black social life walking down the middle of the street – for a minute, but only for a minute, unpoliced, another city gathers, dancing. We know it's there, and here, and real; we know what we can't have happens all the time.[77]

---

[76] Lucille Clifton attributes this quotation to Brooks in an interview with Charles H. Rowell, 'An Interview with Lucille Clifton', *Callaloo* 22.1 (Winter 1999): 56–72 (67).

[77] Fred Moten and Stefano Harney, 'Michael Brown', *Boundary 2* 42 (November 2015): 81–87 (81).

Femi tries to give us both images: the aftermath of violence and the living boy. The first photograph in the book, titled 'N.F.N.C.', is of a hooded figure against a perfectly blue sky. The charcoal-grey hoodie, worn under a black collared jacket, seems to terminate at the edges of the face, but no face can be seen – only a thin white line, and some darker lines, sketching out what seems to be a mask. This figure has obscured its identity, is a blank, and in the context of the book's wake work, seems to loom like the hooded icon of Death itself. But such readings would play into a set of racist assumptions about the hooded Black boy that have been strongly critiqued particularly in the aftermath of the murder of Trayvon Martin, including by Claudia Rankine's *Citizen* – whose cover, from an artwork by David Hammons, similarly presents a blank, empty hood as armour and shroud, symbol of threat and of lynching, anonymity and susceptibility.[78]

Patricia Williams describes hoodies as 'sites of anxiety and secrecy' that 'provide shelter from hostile gaze, yet also the titillation of erotic revelation. They provide a curtain against the world, yet speak simultaneously of oppression and indictment and taboo'.[79] The hoodie is a way of controlling the visibility of the body. No Face No Case – someone who can't be seen can't be held accountable. This interpretation of the hoodie presupposes a malevolent intent. But Femi writes in another poem: 'at the worst times I become invisible / at the worst times I become visible' (3–4). Aligned with the right to opacity guarded by some of Femi's ironic lyrics is the argument made by Bryan Wagner: that 'Blackness suggests a situation in which you are anonymous to yourself. It is a kind of invisibility.'[80] Femi's book includes photographs of other invisible boys. One in a crimson hoodie, only the tip of his nose and lips visible, leans awkwardly with an arched back against an emergency exit sign in a dimly lit hallway (34); a figure in a black North Face jacket and trackies emerges from a brick passageway, their face covered by a wrinkled gold fabric (49), perhaps the same that obscures the face of the first hooded person. That image accompanies a poem on 'Boys in Hoodies', which attests that 'The inside of a hoodie is a veiled nook where a boy pours himself / into a single drop of rain to feed a forest' – though 'the outside world sees this boy as a chainsaw' (48). In the absence of nature that Femi laments across his work, the boy creates a paradisial environment internally, within the folds of his clothing. As Femi explains, 'Often these boys are just as

---

[78] Shermaine M. Jones, '"I Can't Breathe!": Affective Asphyxia in Claudia Rankine's *Citizen: An American Lyric*', *South* 50.1 (2017): 37–45 (40).

[79] Patricia Williams, 'The Luminance of Guilt', *Transition* 113 (2014): 153–170 (167).

[80] Bryan Wagner, *Disturbing the Peace: Black Culture and the Police Power after Slavery* (Cambridge, MA: Harvard University Press, 2009), 1.

delicate as we can ever imagine them to be. They are nourishing to the environment in a way that raindrops are.'[81] But such interpretations also feel like addresses to readers who fear that 'youts will come / for you in the small of the night' – don't worry, the poem assures us, what you read visually as a threat can be transformed through the operation of lyric metaphor into a pastoral interior, a place of safety.

'Just as the hoodie renders identification of its wearer more difficult, the hoodie also provides cover for antiblackness': Mimi Thi Nguyen argues that 'the hoodie makes perceptible the significance of surfaces for a racial optics. Because clothing is both contiguous and not contiguous with what it covers – skin, flesh – it is a mutable boundary that asserts itself within a field of matter, forcing us to confront the intimacy between bodies and things, and the interface between their amalgam and the environment'.[82] That intimacy, I've already argued, is present in Femi's poetics of concrete; it appears also in the architecture of the hoodie. The hoodie is a surface whose depth provokes white middle-class paranoia; it is a space of retreat but also of danger, that can protect or invite scrutiny and persecution. It is a porous surface, at risk of being penetrated by the violence of others, including the police: 'when a knife enters you', 'You will question if you have always been / an empty cove waiting to be filled by another boy's rage' (111). Femi represents this interior as a vulnerable space, skin and fabric insufficiently shielding a body conditioned to accept 'the blade with comfort, / like an inheritance' or birthmark. The boy may feel like he has become concrete, impermeable; however, the hoodie is not armour but softness, an exterior that offers little protection to its vulnerable inside.

These hooded figures present a critique of the cultural capital that predominantly white-owned, middle-class firms continue to make from Black creativity and labour. Presenting entirely as an exterior, an exterior made from fashion, they try to remain illegible: to retain an opacity that resists inspection by the reader's policing imagination. This is a form of self-determination, which takes up the fungibility of Black working-class life to the state and the police, and adopts the presentation of a protective uniformity, creating a shelter within the softness of fabric for the de-individuated external self. Like Femi's poems, these photographs enact different forms of lyric intimacy, relishing each other as generic forms while rejecting the individuation that poetry dramatises in its eroticised privacy.

---

[81] Armitstead, 'Caleb Femi'.
[82] Mimi Thi Nguyen, 'The Hoodie as Sign, Screen, Expectation, and Force', *Source: Signs* 40.4 (Summer 2015): 791–816 (802, 792).

2 Bhanu Kapil

'Like this?' The opening line of Bhanu Kapil's 2020 collection *How to Wash a Heart* invites the reader to give their approval: do you like this?[83] Am I doing it right? Is a poetry like this what you want? Positioned from the first as the judge for whom the speaker performs, the reader shapes the narrative that follows – an account of a brown-skinned, precarious guest within the home of an intrusive host, a poetry of unequal exchange and violation. When the guest, usually a lyric 'I', addresses the host as the intimate 'you', the reader too is interpellated as a performative, hypocritical liberal, whose displays of generosity are part of a disciplinary regime that ends in the guest's deportation. Unlike Femi's poems, which guard the opacity of the individuated subject from a policing gaze behind concrete exteriors and softened, protective interiors, *Heart* lays its protagonist wide open to a probing, intimate curiosity. But like Femi, Kapil also interrogates the sentimental political commitments of middle-class readers, through the topos of hospitality. And, as in *Poor*, the perceived fungibility of Black and brown subjects and the penetration of the private by power struggles situate *Heart* as an often ironic lyric work.

Kapil has, for many years, meditated on 'the axial space between domestic, non-apparent modes of violence and public gestures, murderous gestures, that cannot be revoked', the intersection between public and private trauma.[84] That includes the cost of racialisation and histories of migration, hidden within domestic abuse, addiction, and mental illness. This axial space is the one inhabited by *Heart*'s slender columnar poems. *Heart* is a personalised fable of migration and a political critique of the hypocrisy of liberal charity. The poems hover around twenty lines each, with short verses, dramatic line breaks and enjambments, and relatively simple and direct language. Kapil describes it as 'a very ordinary or banal book'[85] that 'arrived all at once one day, as if it was being dictated by a very clear voice'.[86] But these themes have been the ground zero of Kapil's practice for many years. *The Vertical Interrogation of Strangers* (2001) was constructed from responses by Indian women to prompts asking about their lives. *Humanimal* (2009) revisits the story of 'feral children' Amala and

---

[83] Bhanu Kapil, *How to Wash a Heart* (Liverpool: Pavilion, 2020), 1. Afterwards title is given as *Heart*.

[84] Bhanu Kapil, 'Poetics Statement', in *American Poets in the 21st Century: Poetics of Social Engagement*, ed. Michael Dowdy and Claudia Rankine (Middletown, CT: Wesleyan University Press, 2018), 249.

[85] Amber Pollock, '*How to Wash a Heart*: An Interview with Bhanu Kapil', *Liverpool University Press* blog (27 April 2020): https://liverpooluniversitypress.blog/2020/04/27/how-to-wash-a-heart-an-interview-with-bhanu-kapil/.

[86] 'Open Access: Bhanu Kapil', *Poetry Book Society* blog: www.poetrybooks.co.uk/blogs/news/open-access-bhanu-kapil.

Kamala, girls supposedly raised by wolves in Bengal in the 1920s, exploring the blurry borders of the human and more-than-human as sites of colonial ideology. *Schizophrene* (2011) addresses the epigenetic damage of Partition and the higher incidence of mental illness among migrant populations. *Ban en Banlieue* (2015) is a 'semi-autobiographical novel' about Kapil's childhood in a London suburb and the Southall Riots of 1979. All of these books 'track themes, lived experience and memory related to being a human being in a time in which Far Right rhetoric and practice is resurgent'.[87] They metabolise those histories and spit them back out.

'I think about a monster to think about an immigrant', Kapil writes (*Ban* 78). Whether it's the red cyborg Laloo in *Incubation*, or Ban the 'black' child from Hayes, or Kamala and Amala who were never able to assimilate into the human linguistic and social environment and died young, Kapil's work dramatises processes of exclusion and the impossibility of belonging through figures of exile: the immigrant, cyborg, animal, werewolf, or monster, banned to the wilderness beyond human community and permitted to be killed with impunity.[88] All of these fugitive creatures are also connected to her own history. Kapil has said that 'the choice to become a writer was identical to the choice to leave my culture, my family, my country. I gripped that pen like animal'.[89] Born in London to Punjabi parents who left India around the time of Partition, Kapil emigrated as an adult to the US, where she taught in Colorado, before returning recently to work in Cambridge. She asks: '"What is born in England but is never English?" What grew a tail? What leaned over and rested its hands on its knees?' (*Ban* 21). That question, perennially renewed in racist discourse, echoes Enoch Powell's assertion that 'The West Indian or Indian does not by being born in England, become an Englishman. In law he becomes a United Kingdom citizen by birth; in fact he is a West Indian or an Asian still.'[90] This white supremacist ideology would exclude the migrant and the person of colour from rights and the British community, fix them under a perpetual ban. As the authors of *Empire's Endgame* put it, 'The migrant always remains both racialised and outside of Britain's national story, regardless of the rights granted to Commonwealth and colony subjects by the 1948 British Nationality Act, and

---

[87] Pollock, 'Interview'.

[88] Giorgio Agamben, *Homo Sacer: Sovereign Power and Bare Life*, trans. Daniel Heller-Roazen (Stanford, CA: Stanford University Press, 1995); Grégoire Chamayou, *Manhunts: A Philosophical Theory*, trans. Steven Randall (Princeton, NJ: Princeton University Press, 2010).

[89] Rowland Saifi, 'Unfold Is the Wrong Word: An Interview with Bhanu Kapil', *HTML Giant* (18 April 2012): https://htmlgiant.com/author-spotlight/unfold-is-the-wrong-word-an-interview-with-bhanu-kapil/.

[90] Randall Hansen, *Citizenship and Immigration in Postwar Britain* (Oxford: Oxford University Press, 2000), 188.

the centuries of military, economic, social and political connections forged by empire.'[91] Kapil makes use of the *ostranenie* of avant-garde poetic and performance practices to make a virtue of that political estrangement. Ironically, as her most explicitly lyrical take on migration, *Heart* has also done the most of all Kapil's books to bring her work into the fold of the English culture industry, bringing prizes, media coverage, and a position at the heart of the British academic establishment as a bye-fellow at Churchill College, Cambridge.

Heart draws extensively on Kapil's performances, but it also *is* a performance of sometimes exoticising beauty, trauma, and exilic memory. Staging the politics of migration as a closet drama between two (sometimes three) people, *Heart* weaponises lyric intimacies as perverse and performative displays of power. Conventional lovers are replaced in this book by the fractious dyad of migrant guest and white liberal host, partially complicated by a third presence, a 'brown baby' adopted by the host but mistaken in the world for the guest's child. The lyric interior morphs via the Home Office (in charge of UK immigration) into an actual home where the guest is received, monitored, and eventually expelled. At the same time, the book tests Kapil's faith in the power of lyric to convey 'ancestral vibration' – painful histories, connections and disconnections to the ancestral past, by 'working with sound, phonemes, the light that words give off'.[92] This is *Heart*'s paradoxical, or dialectical, achievement: it uses lyric to critique lyric; intimacy to critique intimacy; and – in Berlant's terms – 'links the instability of individual lives to the trajectories of the collective' through scalar movements between the couple form and the history of nations.

Hospitality and Hostility

Those movements are represented in *Heart* through a language of hospitality that refers specifically to the politics of migration. Jacques Derrida considers hospitality from the same perspective. He argues that 'absolute' hospitality is de-individuating: it makes an offer based not on the identity of the guest, but in honour of their otherness, without making any reciprocal demand.

> Absolute hospitality requires that I open up my home and that I give not only to the foreigner (provided with a family name, with the social status of being a foreigner, etc.), but to the absolute, unknown, anonymous other, and that I give place to them, that I let them come, that I let them arrive, and take place in the place I offer them, without asking of them either reciprocity (entering

---

91 Gargi Bhattacharyya, Adam Elliott-Cooper, Sita Balani, et al., *Empire's Endgame: Racism and the British State* (London: Pluto Press, 2021), 63.

92 'Bhanu Kapil Interviewed by Ivy Johnson', *580 Split* (2018): https://580split.org/interview/interview-with-bhanu-kapil/.

into a pact) or even their names. The law of absolute hospitality commands
a break with hospitality by right, with law or justice as rights.[93]

Instead of a judicial inquiry into the name and nature of the other, absolute
hospitality begins 'with the unquestioning welcome, in a double effacement, the
effacement of the question and the name' as a gesture of tenderness. In *Heart*,
however, hospitality is wretchedly conditional. The host interrogates the guest,
demanding that she disclose her history in specific ways, performing and
aestheticising her trauma in a linear narrative that affirms a redemptive arc
from the abandonment of a violent, exoticised home country to her rescue by the
Global North.

   Derrida is challenging the defensive posture of Western migration policies. In
practice, hospitality can provoke more complicated and antagonistic exchanges.
As Andrew Shyrock observes from his research with Bedouin communities,
allegories between the moral space of household or familial hospitality and
nation-state politics of migration can 'produce morally disturbing results.
Citizens should interact as equals, even when they are not; hosts and guests
cannot interact as equals, even when they are'. Guests don't stay forever;
migrants are expected to behave like good guests, which means assimilation,
eventually transforming into hosts.

> The guest, Jordanians tell me, 'is prisoner of the host.' Visitors are treated
> well, but their mobility is limited. They cannot move freely about the house or
> help themselves to food a drink; they depend on their hosts for protection and
> respect. But guests eventually move on, leaving behind more proverbial
> wisdom: 'The host must fear the guest. When he sits [and shares your
> food], he is company. When he stands [and leaves your house], he is a poet.[94]

The guest in Kapil's book is a prisoner, dependent and constrained by her host's
expectations and demands. Her removal at the book's end further depletes her
power. But she is indeed a poet: she has stories to tell of her own, which survive
her deportation, and this book is her revenge. The host is also a poet, a rival who
rips off her ideas (3), suggesting that beneath her uneasy welcome there is also
jealousy and desire – expressed throughout *Heart* by references to the host's
appetite, a wolfish need to devour the guest's exposed organs.

   Kapil says that *Heart* was inspired by a photograph of a Californian couple
who 'had opened their home to a guest with a precarious visa status. What
caught my attention was the tautness of the muscles around the mouths of these

---

[93] Jacques Derrida, *Of Hospitality*, trans. R. Bowlby (Stanford, CA: Stanford University Press, 2000), 25.

[94] Andrew Shryock, 'Breaking Hospitality Apart: Bad Hosts, Bad Guests, and the Problem of Sovereignty', *The Journal of the Royal Anthropological Institute* 18 (2012): S20–S33 (S23).

hosts. Perhaps they were simply nervous of being photographed. Nevertheless, the soft tissue contraction of those particular muscles are at odds (when visible) to a smile itself'.[95]

The tension Kapil imagines in their faces is a symptom of repressed disgust, which becomes increasingly apparent across the collection as the host's early effort at liberality and repression gives way to outright violence. Kapil's reading of the lines of the face draws on lived experience of 'disgust' as an emotion that lodges in the body of its object: 'You see the facial muscles organise and conceal this expression: fleetingly. You respond.'[96] The racist's 'flinching' and 'almost subliminal facial tic of disgust' inflicts 'a corollary crumping or freezing in the mid-section of the person who absorbs [receives] *what has just happened*', a spasm in the coccyx and jaw. As Frantz Fanon's 'look, a Negro!' scene has insisted, racialisation is not just a feature of the surface of bodies, but a transfer of bodily antagonisms and energies, an introjection that can be felt deep in the nervous system and musculature of the racialised person's body.[97] In an interview, Kapil also reflected on England as a place that 'was in the process of expelling me', and where, 'every day, for a long period of two or three years, my mother was spat on on the train'.[98] A gesture of intimate, contaminating contact, this expectoration is a way of externalising disgust and passing it directly onto the body of the Other.

These experiences and resistance to them manifest in Kapil's deeply embodied poetics. To put it reductively, whereas in Femi's collection the poem is an architecture, in Kapil's work, the labile form of the body gives a structure to the 'syntax' of the poem. The body's flinches, contractions, stalling, 'throes, convulsions, peristalsis' afflict poetry's 'acoustic arcs' and staggering paragraphs. In *Heart*, this feels like a quiet, subdued body is carefully preserving its resources in the poems' prosody, taking measured breaths to stave off panic. Kapil says that poetry can 'work very intensely with the sensations and textures of colonisation, the half-lives of a colonial impact, but also – through the work of rhyme or sound – to also be the means by which inherited forms of trauma, in their non-verbal states, might also: move through'.[99] Rhyme and sound echo the ancestral vibrations and the spasms of trauma that get locked in the body and allows them to be metabolised and released. Poetry is a home where (in Femi's words) *'all / of your unwanted*

---

[95] Pollock, 'Interview'.   [96] Kapil, 'Poetics Statement', 249.

[97] Frantz Fanon, *Black Skin, White Masks*, trans. Charles Lam Markmann (London: Pluto Press, 2008), 82.

[98] Stephanie Luczajko, 'An Interview with Bhanu Kapil', *Tinge Magazine* (Autumn 2011): www.tingemagazine.org/an-interview-with-bhanu-kapi/.

[99] Pollock, 'Interview'.

memories' (*Poor* 99) can be kept, and a method for activating those memorial tremors in order to let them go. This, too, is part of the dialectical work that *Heart* undertakes: process and release, through the figure of the migrant who is processed and detained.

Butchery and Passivity

At a performance at the ICA in London on 19 June 2019 that gave *How to Wash a Heart* its title, Kapil introduces her reading:

> To open up the cavity of the thorax – the chest – how do you say? To open up the heart space and to then remove the heart is a sacrificial mode. How to wash a heart. It means that someone is no longer here. I began to think, Who's not here? Then I realised: it's the ancestor, the one who came just before.[100]

The performance is a way of grieving and dreaming for the ancestors, she says. Their absent presence is frozen in time and integrated in the body as intergenerational trauma. But by removing it, making it a 'show', the ancestral heart can also be freed of its burdens and trauma can be metabolised. Vowing that it is the last time she will read from *Schizophrene*, Kapil selects an image of women 'tied to the border trees' with their stomachs cut out – an image of the ghastly violence of Partition that her mother 'repeated to me at many bedtimes of my own childhood' (*Ban* 40), mixed together with stories from the Ramayana. Adapting a performance titled *Good Blood* by Lygia Pape,[101] and perhaps referring to Alan Kaprow's *Fluids* installation, Kapil pours hot water into a bowl of red ice cubes (in the chapbook *Threads*, she described ice as 'a public form of whiteness that does not melt but freezes'[102]), which she later decants as meltwater into the street. This translation of the frozen image of trauma into a liquidity that can be dispersed in the public way is a ritual act of mourning, like the libations poured out in Femi's poems. It is also a reactivation of the energy captured in the ice-bound ancestral 'vibration' that allows it to be shared.

Kapil's performance at the ICA is referenced directly throughout *Heart*. 'How to wash a heart: / Remove it. / *Animal or ice?*'. The latter is 'the curator's question', answered as the speaker resolves 'to plunge my forearms / Into the red ice / That is already melting / In the box' (5). But within *Heart*'s intimate domestic setting, the removed and exposed heart is both a sign of the guest's vulnerability in a dangerous place and a parodic literalisation of lyric feeling, the

---

[100] Bhanu Kapil, Live Recording, ICA (19 June 2019): www.ica.art/live/how-to-wash-a-heart.

[101] Peter Howarth, 'Lightning Conductor', *London Review of Books* 44.11 (9 June 2022): www.lrb.co.uk/the-paper/v44/n11/peter-howarth/lightning-conductor.

[102] Bhanu Kapil, 'Avert the Icy Feeling: Fourteen Notes on Race and Creative Writing (with Bonus Trauma Loop)', *Threads* (London: Clinic, 2018), 51.

rendering of private interiority as spectacle. The host threatens to 'devour' her heart and internal organs that are 'exposed to view' (3); the reader is also suspected of wishing to consume the heart's naked confessions, becoming in the process a predatory animal.[103]

Kapil remembers reading William Congreve at university: 'Writing as revenge. That stayed with me for a long time: literature as butcher's shop.'[104] *Heart* alludes to earlier performances in which Kapil made use of the accoutrements of butchery. These include a butcher's table (3) and a butcher's hook, which also becomes the hook through which value is extracted from the host's adopted daughter:

> Verbally, you state egalitarian
> Ideals.
> Financially, you hook
> That brown baby
> Up. (39)

With its stuttering rhythms, the poem isolates the host's 'ideals' as a bare word set alone on its line, with nothing to prop it up or elaborate it. The parallel between the verbal and the financial exposes the host's hypocrisy, which is also (through the directness of its address) the reader's own. The true nature of these supposedly egalitarian ideals becomes apparent in the host's milking of the 'brown baby' for social or other capital. That baby is hooked 'up' as the sentence gradually climbs down the page, each syntactical unit deposited carefully and arduously, slowing down time as the baby is sucked rather than sucking. Kapil has said commas and semicolons are like 'butcher's hooks; sites of visceral comprehension. A way, also, to point away from the forward movement of time in a narrative; towards history. That meat shop. Writing a sentence is thus a way to think about land mass, colonial history and the body at the same time'.[105] The commas after the adverbs in this quotation are hooks that string up the joints of history, bringing together the racialisation of the baby, the rhetoric of liberalism, and the economics of extractive capitalism.

Kapil has also fantasised about writing a book 'on a butcher's table in New Delhi: the shopfront open to the street, a bare light bulb swinging above the table and next to it a hook' (*Ban* 42). For her 'butcher's shop' and 'meat sack' performances in the US in 2011 and 2013, Kapil crawled into a red sack on

---

[103] On the trope of being 'eaten alive' in Kapil's work, see Eunsong Kim, 'Perpetual Writing, Institutional Rupture, and the Performance of No: The Poetics of Bhanu Kapil', *American Poets in the 21st Century*, 251–266 (255–256).

[104] 'Profiles in Poetics & Linguistics: Bhanu Kapil', *Women's Quarterly Conversation* (13 November 2015): https://womensquarterlyconversation.com/category/bhanu-kapil/. Kapil may be thinking of Congreve's famous remark in *The Mourning Bride* (1697): 'Heaven has no rage, like love to hatred turned, / Nor Hell a fury, like a woman scorned.'

[105] Johnson, 'Interview', *580 Split*.

top of a butcher's table. Recordings of *Schizophrene* played in the background as the audience watched, like voyeurs or witnesses to a scene of terrible violence, through the window. This positioning is related to the 'you' addressed in *Heart*, who is both looking into the scene of coercive domesticity with an eroticised curiosity, and a participant in its violence. These performances were reckonings with personal and political history. Recollecting the 1979 riot, Kapil has said: 'I am not sure if I am a poet anymore. Sometimes I feel like meat slipping off a wet table instead. Sometimes I feel like the butcher. Sometimes I feel like the city. And sometimes I feel like everything at once, rotating and flexing on the butcher's table: right there in the window of my childhood home.'[106] The butcher's table is a metaphor for historicity, a site of remembering and dismembering, where the self becomes jointed, doing and done to, and all while – like the washed heart – in the public gaze. There is both risk and plangency in Kapil's desire to write a book in these conditions, to describe and become 'the body as meat seen through a window by neighbors, throbbing, gesticulating, pre-meat perhaps – in a scene of domestic or sexual violence displayed to the street'.[107] Trapping herself on the altar of the table within the public gaze, Kapil makes visible the way the animal is captured, dismembered, and consumed. She refers the performance to the violated bodies and 'organ meat' 'shed onto the jungle floor (carpet) during an act of wartime or in-country (home) violence'. Forcing spectators to look directly at 'those blood-soaked materials', her ritual performance is both a calling to memory, and an act of revenge.[108]

As Carol J. Adams has argued, there is a connection between the animalisation of women and the sexualisation and feminisation of animals that sustains material and symbolic forms of violence against both.[109] Kapil's performances mourn and rage against that violence. In a memorial ritual performed in 2014,

---

[106] Bhanu Kapil, 'Stories Are Chemical', *Poetry Foundation* (9 April 2012): www.poetryfoundation.org/harriet-books/2012/04/stories-are-chemical.

[107] Katherine Sanders, 'Bhanu Kapil', *Bomb Magazine* (22 September 2011): https://bombmagazine.org/articles/bhanu-kapil/.

[108] Sanders, 'Bhanu Kapil'. In her collaboration with Sandeep Parmar for the volume *Threads*, Kapil recalls a story she was told by a relative: 'We heard from our neighbours. They hid us. They helped us. The family on the other side of them .... slaughtered .... all of them .... the five daughters .... and one night our neighbours were on their roof, sleeping, and two of their own daughters, maybe seven and nine, saw, on the roof of that family, the family who had died, those five sisters, the daughters who had been .... chopped up .... dancing, dressed in white, all white, salwar chemise, dupatta, everything, white. They saw it with their own eyes and woke up their parents. But then the girls, dancing, hand in hand, in a circle, singing a beautiful song, a quawaal, were gone.' Parmar with Kapil, 'Lyric Violence, the Nomadic Subject and the Fourth Space', 17.

[109] Carol J. Adams, *The Sexual Politics of Meat: A Feminist-Vegetarian Critical Theory* (London: Bloomsbury, 2015).

Kapil lay down in the place in South Delhi where, in December 2012, Jyoti Singh Pandey, who was gang-raped and tortured, lay for forty minutes before anyone called the police. Kapil strewed sindoor powder and peacock ore (a sparkly, multicoloured crystal also known as bornite) on the ground, her body framed by candles and flowers by attending activists. In this performance, Kapil chose 'to sacralize the space against its own obscenity', in Lauren Berlant's words.[110] As Kapil asks in *Heart*, echoing the 'chalk outlines' in Femi's poem 'Flowering': 'Is a poet / An imperial dissident, or just / An outline / Of pale blue chalk?' (29). Does poetic resistance do anything, or just trace a bare line around the site of violence? Her sacred drawing threatens to dissolve into the police's chalked outline at the crime scene: another absence marking the site of misogynist violence, or a smudged blank soon to be washed from the city's memory.

Ana Mendieta's 'Rape Scene' (1973) – a series of performance works responding to the rape and murder of a student at the University of Iowa, in which Mendieta leaned over her kitchen table, bound and naked with her underwear around her ankles and her legs and ass covered in animal blood – influenced Kapil's butcher's table and ritual for Pandey. Her performances also reference Mendieta's 'Silueta' series, where the artist imprinted female forms on the earth from materials including 'flowers, tree branches, moss, gunpowder, and fire, occasionally combined with animals' hearts or handprints that she branded directly into the ground'.[111] On one occasion, Kapil lay down, then filmed 'the outline a body leaves, re-filled with marigolds and tiny oil lamps'; this brief performance, no more than five minutes long, was intended to open out into 'planetary or evacuated time' – the 'span of time from Partition in 1948' through to the present, bleeding outwards in space and time 'across agricultural and urban thresholds, seemingly forever, until, serrated by Turkmenistan, by the concrete edifices of Akshabad, and the sharp mountain range beyond the city'.[112] The poem enacts the kind of time lag described by Homi K. Bhabha, in which 'the linear, progressive time of modernity' is slowed down, the present brought to a standstill in astonishment, the dead symbols of the past made present. 'Where these temporalities touch contingently, their spatial boundaries metonymically overlapping, at that moment their margins are lagged, sutured, by the indeterminate articulation of the "disjunctive" present. *Time-lag keeps*

---

[110] Lauren Berlant, *On the Inconvenience of Other People* (Durham, NC: Duke University Press, 2022), 164.

[111] Ana Mendieta, 'Untitled: Silueta Series', *Guggenheim* collection online: www.guggen heim.org/artwork/5221.

[112] Lisa Birman with Bhanu Kapil, *Trickhouse* 4 (Spring 2009): www.trickhouse.org/vol4/inter view/birman&kapil.html.

alive the making of the past', Bhabha argues.[113] I'll say more about the disjunctive presence of the past in *Heart* later in this section; but these sutured, disjointed parts of time are related both to Kapil's desire to help the ancestors to arrive, and her metaphors of butchery.

Kapil's prone performances have also commented on the securitisation of borders. 'I want to lie down in the place I am from: on the street I am from', 'As I did, on the border of Pakistan and India: the two Punjabs', she writes in *Ban* (31), re-siting the violent history of that border to the street in London's Southall and its distinct racial politics. The body prostrate on the border takes rest, gives up, and makes of itself an obstacle. This position of passivity in the face of power and history, which is surrender and resistance and self-care, is recreated in the positions taken by Ban. Walking home from school down the Uxbridge Road in 1979, Ban hears the sound of breaking glass, a premonition of the oncoming race riot. 'Knowing that either way she's done for – she lies down to die' (*Ban* 20). It seems a bleak, hopeless end. But in Stoic terms, Ban's deliberate surrendering to death is a way out of her subjection: she chooses to go, to become still, an object that cannot be further hurt. Following Agamben's writing on the *homo sacer*, Kapil conceives of Ban at that moment as socially dead, but recovering her sovereignty by willingly surrendering her life.[114] Ban claims her own agency through radical passivity.

As anyone knows who has attempted to pick up a toddler who decides to flop, the body that lies down can manifest an extraordinary heaviness, an outsized, wilful resistance to the powers that try to make it comply. Kapil remembers as a child lying down in Epping Forest, 'where King Henry VIII had his hunting grounds' (*Ban* 41), enacting a humanimal liminality. The prone person makes contact with the earth in a form that is shared with crawling and slithering animals. *Heart* also references these lying-down performances, and the revision of perspective and condition that they induce. '*Contact nature / On all fours*, said the counsellor, / Slipping off her chair onto the floor' (*Heart* 6); 'Sometimes I lie on the earth face down / To connect / With its copper plate' (17). The guest's postures and rolfing movements generate new thoughts: 'like a baby crawling on the bumpy / Carpet, am I my own / Mother, actually?' (10). Crawling is a significant developmental milestone, building not only the core strength and coordination of the child, but also their experiential knowledge of the world. Crawling performances translate the infantile position of the guest into one of empowering proximity to the earth and its knowledge.

---

[113] Homi K. Bhabha, *The Location of Culture* (London: Routledge, [1994] 2004), 364.
[114] Agamben, *Homo Sacer*, 8–12.

Lying down, in Amy De'Ath's reading of *Ban*, signals 'a desire to be close to the world, or get to know it, both in the material sense of land and landscape – the solid earth and its historicity – and in terms of the real abstractions of global capital that emerge from and determine this physical landscape'; it offers 'a powerful gesture of solidarity with the horizontal figures of racialised dead women'.[115] In Sarah Dowling's analysis of Kapil's prostrate figures in *Ban en Banlieue*, the action of lying down is 'not oriented toward notions of recognition, redress, or repair, but . . . motivated by a desire to be with, to be near, and to be like those who have suffered and are suffering'.[116] Lying down can be a form of tenderness and intimacy. Kapil tells the story of such an act:

> Swami Ramananda lay down with a man who was about to die and described an orchard of lemon trees, pomegranate trees, vividly describing it, and continued speaking even when the man had passed. In this category, would be hospice workers and all the people who work with refugees, with people whose bodies have suffered in ways that we would not tolerate, even for a moment. We would scream.[117]

Dowling connects Kapil's prostrations to the die-ins held by ACT-UP and other political movements; they might also remind us of the *tang ping* or lying-flat movement that was taken up in China as a resistance to relentless work in 2022. But as Dowling notes, 'in Kapil's book the posture does not contribute to the making of a collective' (150); 'the self-contained, individual body demonstrates the repetitive quality of violence, without constituting a collective, and without preserving its own individual subjectivity while striking the pose' (155). It is a distillation of refusal that leaves Ban 'a passive and inert object, prone at the side of the road' (151), enacting her objectification by racism as she awaits her death.

True Stories and Counterfeits

But other forms of more subtle resistance are possible, and in *Heart*, these are expressed by the guest's refusal or inability to act with total decorum, and her reluctance to perform her history in the forms required by the host. She holds onto her own artistry while performing minor private and aesthetic disruptions. The host's 'desire for art / That comes from a foreign / Place' (4) demands specific narratives:

---

[115] Amy De'Ath, 'L(a)ying Down in the Banlieu', *Mute* (21 September 2016): www.metamute.org/editorial/articles/laying-down-banlieue.

[116] Sarah Dowling, 'Supine, Prone, Precarious', in *Poetics and Precarity*, ed. Myung Mi Kim and Cristanne Miller (Albany, NY: SUNY Press, 2018), 145–160 (148).

[117] Birman with Kapil, *Trickhouse*.

> Tell me about your long journey,
> You said, that
> First day. Are your children
> White? (19)

Again, the reader is included in this 'you' who wants the 'hook' of a compelling narrative of suffering and escape. The poem accentuates our desires with its careful lineation. 'White' is self-sufficient, positioned on its own line (like 'Ideals' in the quotation on page 20 of this Element); it foregrounds the host's racial fixation and mimics fascist discourses around the 'great replacement' of white populations. This painful non-sequitur gives the lie to the host's seeming interest in the story of the journey. In response, the guest describes a river on which poets 'loved to soar in its pellid / Current' (19), the adjective reaching towards a self-consciously poetic register; she goes on to describe an Orientalist landscape filled with snakes and poets sitting on the banks who sing 'a song called *Gugga*' (19) (the Punjabi Gogaji, a folk deity worshipped for his ability to protect worshippers against poisonous snakes). She performs lyric. But her exotic pastorals are rejected by the host:

> No, you said.
> I want to hear what happened afterwards
> Not before.

It's not the homeland that interests the host/us, but the trauma of exodus. When the guest tries to comply, her 'catastrophic representation' (14) is also rejected as not fitting the host's demands for clarity, 'linearity', just enough detail but not too much. The guest's refusal or inability to comply with these generic and narrative constraints has a 'cost' (34); she anticipates a punishment for failing to conform to the aesthetic needs of the host. The guest is reluctant to perform any more. Though she initially resists the requirement 'to beautify our collective trauma' (2), to aestheticise her struggle in the way she does in the Gugga song passage, she 'trains' herself to respond to the host's criticism and supply the requisite imagery, even if much of what she tells the host is a series of 'fake' stories (25).

That some of those fakes might include the stories in this book – 'the footprint / Of an ancient god / Embellished with vermillion / Powder / And marigolds / Every morning for a thousand years' (25), the snake charming poets and drought-cancelling magic fish – aligns the readerly 'you' with the host as someone who demands, and critiques, the offering of Orientalist narratives by those who are accepted as 'guests' into the domain of Anglophone lyric. The book's second section dwells on family memories and myths of origin from before the guest's emigration. These memories provide a 'backdrop / Of eternal time', hazy ancient temporalities that are contrasted with the diurnal struggle for survival of the guest within the adoptive home. The guest recollects her grandfather fermenting 'yoghurt / With rose petals / And sugar then buried it / In the roots of a mango tree' (11): 'Come June', it was 'the sweetest fruit I have ever tasted'. This image of nourishment contrasts with the wolfish appetite of the host, but also exemplifies what Sandeep Parmar describes as 'the expectation from a mainly white British readership that poets of colour must grapple with the longing of exile and alienation by fixating on exotic tropes (a confluence of saris, mangoes, pomegranates, arranged marriages)'.[118]

In just this way, the guest's stories depict a verdant family holding, with an orchard where saffron and pomegranate grew. The fruit conveys not life but death, as in the Greek myth that associates it with Hades, its ruby fruit reminiscent of clotted blood. The plot is also contaminated by a bloody history: the dry well 'is where they threw / the bodies / Come August' (11), a possible reference to stories of women who jumped into wells to escape rape and murder during Partition. But as Kapil writes elsewhere, 'The ghosts and monsters in our stories are seated at the bottom of the dank well, throats extended, mouths open ready to receive whatever's poured down there.' The well is the poisoned source of nourishment, of growth, a deep and mysterious hole; the throat of the monstrous dead or migrant is a kind of well (*Threads* 21).

Parallelism links the sweet smell of the mango with the smell of the rotting bodies, such that the question, 'Can you find your way home / By smell?' is not one only of nostalgia about returning to a site of plenty and pleasure through the exercise of an animalistic skill, but also to a site where 'the flowers of the mango tree / . . . once concealed / A kill'. These horror stories fulfil 'your' expectations. The kill is concealed within the flowers of the mango tree and within the fragrant lines of the poem, where the memories of death, the fear of being devoured by the host, and the wish to kill her in revenge for the atrocities the guest has experienced singly and communally, are latent behind images of 'civilised' domesticity, and the exquisitely patient rhythms created by Kapil's line breaks.

Heart laments that 'My ancestral line/ Was decimated, / For example, / One hot night' (29). The guest may be able to write her poetic lines here, but the ancestral line has been destroyed – and this is merely an 'example' of a larger historical truth. Tragic loss is rendered generic, a marker of many migrants' experiences of urgent departure: 'When our neighbors / Said go, we fled'; her grandfather burned his notebooks, the family 'lost all our possessions' (13),

---

[118] Sandeep Parmar, 'Not a British Subject: Race and Poetry in the UK', *LA Review of Books* (6 December 2015): https://lareviewofbooks.org/article/not-a-british-subject-race-and-poetry-in-the-uk/.

including 'Silk, rubies, scripture / Written from right / To left. A shirt made from raw cotton', earrings, Arden Shakespeares, 'The nurse's cape I wore to university', a painting of English houses, 'Oh, everything' (35). Leaving home, abandoning both indigenous treasures and the relics of a British colonial education, the speaker feels 'a strange relief / To see my home explode in the rearview mirror' (13). That rearview mirror offers an orientation towards the past, which can be seen within the frame of reflection, rather than gazed at directly; like the small enclosures of the lyric poem, it offers only a small portion of the scene, not the disaster in its full scale.

The guest says, 'I come from a country / All lime-pink on the soggy map' (7), its colour signifying that her country of origin was part of the British Empire. *Heart* alludes to atrocities committed during Partition and its aftermath: 'The stories in my family are all about people being beheaded, gutted – the evisceration of the female body, glimpsed – and so on. What people did, what they saw. Post-Partition. Those stories have been inherited, culturally, as a kind of domestic and gender violence – in the communities I lived in or belonged to or am from.'[119] Rana Dasgupta has written:

> every Indian Partition family tells the same stories: the armed Muslims descending in hordes on terrified households, the women jumping into wells rather than be dishonoured, the rivers of blood, the miraculous escapes of babies overlooked in the slaughter, the villages where 'they did not leave any girl' ... even as all facts receded, the residual trauma, like DDT in the food chain, became more concentrated with time.[120]

This violence – which, as Dasgupta does not specify, was also perpetrated by Hindus against Muslim communities – targeted both groups' 'reproductive potential: not only indiscriminate slaughter, but also the repeated exposure of unborn foetuses, the ceremonial display of castrated penises – and rape on a colossal scale, whose purpose was genetic subjugation' (190). In Dasgupta's analysis, these events still leave a traumatic blight on Delhi, hidden literally in the city's stones and earth.

The bodies in the well, the smell of rot mixed with the mango flowers: history as it is narrated in *Heart* mixes with wistful exoticism and the confusions of dream. Ancestors appear in horrific visions: a grandmother 'face down / In a cave, immersed / In the lightly flowing water'; a headless man who 'Span my body / From a rusted hook' (42). The butcher's hook reappears, turning bodies into carcasses prepped for consumption. In the relative calm of her host nation, and in these poems, the guest is hung up for inspection. And the book provokes

---

[119] 'Profiles in Poetics & Linguistics', *Women's Quarterly Conversation*.
[120] Rana Dasgupta, *Capital: The Eruption of Delhi* (Edinburgh: Canongate, 2015), 194.

questions about the consumption of all these stories of violence and its antithesis. Is this how we like our migrant narratives – 'like this'? While telling these catastrophic stories may feel like a personal and political compulsion, a way of dreaming and grieving with and for the ancestors, the guest's performance is also responding to the reader's 'desire for art' and generic expectations. Like Femi resisting the transformation of the trauma of Grenfell into 'pub chatter', Kapil accentuates the white reader's desire for beautified trauma not only by examining its narration, but by producing allegories of erotic intimacy that capitalise on lyric's fragile logics of authenticity and address.

Intrusive Intimacies

The host displays the guest for the neighbourhood, making her a spectacle of the host's liberality. But the host's private face is very different. 'When the front door is closed', the axial space between public and private is where the violence of whiteness accumulates. The host demands a fateful and disturbing intimacy from the guest as part of her regimen of control. Sometimes she leaves the guest's door open; other times she locks the guest in, making tangible the guest's mannerly constraint within the house. When the host reads the guest's diary aloud, the guest asks: 'Was this the moment / I became / An alien form?' (41): here again, as across Kapil's work, the immigrant is made to seem a monster, werewolf, or cyborg. The guest is forbidden from having any privacy, like an animal in a zoo or abattoir. This extends to her sexual life. In one poem she invites a lover back to shred 'my dress ... / And my life / Too', in a self-determined act of *jouissance* that contrasts with the life shredded by exile; but the episode ends with the host at the door issuing a polite instruction: '*Listen. / We didn't agree / To this*' (38). The host, trivial in her pyjamas, tries to enforce the fiction that a balanced, contractual relation has been violated, one premised on mutual agreement – that the guest in her desires is misbehaving. The host wants to regulate the guest's behaviour while maintaining a liberal pretence of equality. But her resistance to the intrusion of the guest's desire shows how unsettled she has been by the guest's passionate need for a 'you' who could tear her life to pieces. The guest chooses another you: not 'you' the host or reader, but a lover, a rival to the host's animal appetite, who competes with the host's desire to consume the guest's exposed organs and is invited in.

The host insists on sexualising the guest on her own terms. Her regulation of the guest's sexual behaviour is part of an intrusive hygienic regime. The host buys 'pretty bras' for the guest (26); she sets out shampoo for the guest saying, 'What's mine is yours' with 'a sweet smile' (37). But this generosity has other motives. She affronts the guest: 'I can smell your body / Odor. / I can smell your vagina. / Are you wearing your genitals / As a brooch?', and sets out 'a douche / And the yellow bottle / Of medicated powder' as a 'gift' (37). Even in the supposed safety of her home, the host perpetuates a violation that begins in 'the facility' where individuals are forced to 'disrobe' (28) – not removing the dress shredded in sexual ecstasy, but stripped by bureaucratic force. In one rare moment in which the guest is interpellated as 'you', flipping the positionality, the state takes on the rapacious first person for its enunciation. The guest is forced to internalise its message: 'You are a sexual object, I have a right / To sexualise you. / You are not an individual. / You are here / For my entertainment' (14). The reader may also take pleasure in the spectacle as 'entertainment', becoming a voyeur whose pleasure is anticipated in the book's opening line – 'like this?' The question opens up the possibility that, as in the recitation of trauma and exoticism, these scenes of intimate abuse are command performances that de-individuate the guest and force her to conform to standards set by whiteness.

So long as the guest behaves like 'a treasured pet' (30), she is acceptable, and fed 'salty cream'. But when she deviates from that model, she is disciplined. Small infractions in 'guarded / Rooms' create an atmosphere of fear (31): a drawer that's not pushed in, a wet towel left on the banister. When the guest breaks a vase, the host 'went crazy', and later 'refused to say a word' (24). The host's behaviour devolves from passive aggression into plain aggression: 'You bang the cup down / By my sleepy head' (8). She has become the bad mother, whose resentment retracts every caring gesture she may once have made. Finally, the poem concludes with a scream that breaks the cool self-control of the host. The scream passes between the book's protagonists – guest, host, daughter – as an expression of the host's anger or revenge, the daughter's loss of a brown-skinned comrade, and the guest's response to her violent extraction by the Department of Repatriation:

> There's a knock on the door.
> There's a hand on my arm.
> Your daughter is screaming.
> . . . There's a break in the scream.
> The scream is mine.
> My scream is at hand. (44)

In this final poem, most lines are end-stopped, the sudden intrusion of state violence causing fragmentation in the speaker's observations and a jerking, arrested rhythm. Gripped by trauma and dissociation, the guest is at first unaware if the hand or the scream is her own, before claiming it as her violent articulation of a need that breaks the constraints placed upon her by the host's etiquette. She sees the host exchange a glance with an enforcement officer. The moment interrupts the pseudo-intimacy of her connection with the host and hands the guest over to an agency that will exercise its power without the veil of liberal generosity.

Heart offers the reader a parodic version of lyric intimacy. Taking place within the private space of the host's home, a privacy made public both as a liberal spectacle for the neighbours' sake and by the intrusions of state power when the guest is extracted, the book maps geopolitical histories of colonialism, migration, violence, and racialisation onto the couple form and the intimate I/ thou address that typifies lyric. The host's disappointment with the guest's narrations is a powerful display of the way the Black and brown lyric 'I' is an other. The balance of erotic power between I and you, guest and host, is tipped violently away from the lyric self by the state. In this sense, the book shares Elizabeth Povinelli's perception that

> the intimate couple is a key transfer point between, on the one hand, liberal imaginaries of contractual economics, politics, and sociality, and, on the other, liberal forms of power in the contemporary world. Love, as an intimate event, secures the self-evident good of social institutions, social distributions of life and death, and social responsibilities for those institutions and distributions. If you want to locate the hegemonic home of liberal logic and aspirations, look to love in settler colonies.[121]

Looking at settler colonialism and its aftermaths as an intimate event, *Heart* asks us to acknowledge that the couple form is as perverse as a border. Perhaps, returning to Berlant, there are 'no alternative plots' that can 'bypass the couple or the life narrative it generates'. But Kapil's work resonates with 'the energy of attachment [that] has no designated place' or canon, that has been displaced and continues to vibrate.

Throughout the book, Kapil makes reference to the host as a bad mother and remembers the good and bad parenting of the speaker's own family as she strives to mother herself, rendered infantile by her predicament. The guest and host are locked in a domestic drama of sexual repression, jealousy, and hygienic regulation, worrying about what the neighbours think, and tending anxiously to their property, which includes the 'brown baby' whom a waitress mistakes for the guest's own child. They are, in other words, a fairly conventional family. The book's critique of the conditional hospitality offered by liberal metropoles remains active so long as the reader maintains the awareness that within this family is condensed a multitude and their histories: that this is an allegory, 'for example', in which the private sphere is not a refuge from the state's domination but its epitome.

---

[121] Povinelli, *The Empire of Love*, 17.

That allegory is narrated in the language of lyric feeling, memories, desire, and erotic intimacy, things that get awkward when bodies accustomed to lying in bedrooms lie down on borders. In *Heart*, lyric is a mode of real and parodic intimacy, object and method of critique. The poem is a repository of traumatic memory and, through rhythm as an approximation of ancestral vibration, a mechanism for its release. It is an escape from national histories and a site of their condensation. The guest performs beautiful lyrical scenes (of doubtful authenticity) for the host and for the reader and is put on display by the host and for the reader, 'like this', but these spectacles do not finally undermine the poem's witness to the truth of embodied experiences. The one who hangs her heart up on the butcher's hook has faith that the organ is more than just a cut of meat or dead metaphor. With tense patience, the poem's razor-sharp lineation 'conceals a kill'. Like hospitality, the couple form or the nation-state, lyric is ruined but still needful.

3 Juliana Spahr

(How) can poetry create the conditions for us to be together? Where in Femi's work the lyric subject is collectivised for its pleasure and protection, and in Kapil's the loneliness of the migrant subject makes her more vulnerable, in the poetry of Juliana Spahr, anarchic and revitalising assemblies take shape as crowds, dreams, and grammars. Anti-war marches and the Beloved as numerous 'yous' in *This Connection of Everyone With Lungs* (2005); 'they' who interrogate their participation in settler colonialism in *The Transformation* (2007); the carnival of erotic solidarity that ends *An Army of Lovers* (2013); Occupy encampments in *That Winter the Wolf Came* (2015) – Spahr's poems imagine a plural subject beyond the isolation of lyric personhood.[122] Collectivity flashes out in spaces and temporalities of possibility, flares of multiplicity to think and act within regimes of capitalist oppression, or what 'Some Oakland Antagonists' referred to in the aftermath of Occupy as 'a brief and chaotic glimpse of insurrectionary horizons that closed as quickly as they opened'.[123] Moving across that horizon, Spahr imagines 'the bodies of friends in the crowds of various cities, feel[s] moments of connection with the mass as

---

[122] Juliana Spahr, *This Connection of Everyone with Lungs* (Berkeley, CA: University of California Press, 2005); Juliana Spahr, *The Transformation* (Berkeley, CA: Atelos, 2007); Juliana Spahr and David Buuck, *An Army of Lovers* (San Francisco, CA: City Lights, 2013); Juliana Spahr, *That Winter the Wolf Came* (Oakland, CA: Commune Editions, 2015).

[123] Some Oakland Antagonists, 'The Rise and Fall of the Oakland Commune', *CrimethInc.* (August 2013): https://crimethinc.com/2013/09/10/after-the-crest-part-ii-the-rise-and-fall-of-the-oakland-commune.

I imagine it down to individuals' (*This Connection* 60). Affective bonds are a way of particularising, identifying with, and making space for each other in mass uprisings. In her work, poetry extends its solidarity across fantasied networks to individual friends joined in political desire, as well as to what Timothy Morton calls ecological beings. This, in Morton's sense, is beauty: 'a feeling of unconditional solidarity with things, with everything, with anything'.[124] Sending poetic love letters to anything, including that which poisons us, Spahr expands lyric's erotic intimacy of the two (plus reader) to encompass the desire of and for the multiple. Her radical politics incorporates a faith in and critique of lyric that allies her with the poets discussed thus far.

Across the work of this US poet, togetherness happens in bed, in the streets, in poems and the sea and the forest. Imaginative movement is possible because the poet can put her body almost anywhere – a condition that is not shared by Femi's speakers or Kapil's guest. Spahr's poetry attends, in Berlant's phrase, 'to the glances, gestures, encounters, collaborations, or fantasies that have no canon', by returning them to the fold of lyric intimacy with their plurality intact. But where for Femi the love of mandem has a selectivity based on class, culture and origin, Spahr's multiplying affections extend outward from chosen comrades to many humans and more-than-human others. Spahr, whose position as a white woman in a settler-colonialist state enables her to engage with the police on different terms from Femi's youths or Kapil's guest, is differently impacted by the individuation that arises from surveillance and carcerality. She acknowledges as much: 'I am unwilling to give up desire. I am unwilling to abandon connection. I am unwilling to not be occupied. But I was born into the position of the colonizer not the reverse.'[125] Her poems acknowledge the inescapable complicity of privileged subjects in exploitation but remain committed to a principle of solidarity that extends outward through lyric's intimacies. Like Femi and Kapil, she is invested in an (albeit détourned) version of lyric intimacy, expanded from the couple form but still founded in erotic companionship. In times of crisis, 'I need models of intimacy that are full of acquaintance and publics; that are declarations of collective culture and connective agency. And I need those models to also leave room for individuals, to respect their multiple "onlys."'[126]

As they itemise the devastation of nature and the violence of the state, Spahr's poems also seek ways to add 'the phrase the principle of relation' (*Wolf* 29) to

---

[124] Timothy Morton, *Humankind: Solidarity with Non-human People* (London: Verso, 2017), 56.

[125] Joel Bettridge, 'Conversation with Juliana Spahr', *How2* 2.3 (Spring 2005): www.asu.edu/pipercwcenter/how2journal/archive/online_archive/v2_3_2005/current/workbook/spa/media/spa.pdf.

[126] Juliana Spahr, 'Poetry in a Time of Crisis', *Poetry Project Newsletter* 189 (2002).

inventories of destruction. That principle, which has been elaborated by Édouard Glissant as a willingness to conceive of a totality but renounce 'any claims to sum it up or possess it',[127] could be partly construed as a desire for kinship whose forms are not dictated by property rights. Indeed, Spahr's movement from familial (familiar) arrangements, even unconventional ones, to national and global affections, is not far distant from many confessional poets.[128] But for Spahr, 'the principle of relation' within chosen families is just one kind of intimacy adduced from the myriad intricate ways that human subjects are embedded in larger environments. Spahr tries to attend to these multiple points of connection without lapsing into possessive individualism: to assemble not through lyric empathies, but through an *apathetic* (in the Stoic sense) and flat style that recognises bodies as material forms, human and more-than-human, lively and static, mineral and vegetable, all linked by air and earth and chemicals.

These connections point towards both the cruelty of the present and a communist horizon, a community (Spahr imagines) 'in which what one took from or gave to the social store was entirely voluntary and regulated by nothing so much as one's sense of belonging to a community', in which 'each individual would present as absolute singularity, as specificity belonging to no general category, a unique actualization of social possibilities', needing no recognition or pursuit of distinction. No stratifications of identity would interpose between the absolute particularity of the person and the absolute generality of the whole. The unique subject would be liberated from type or genre; their relation to the community would be regulated not by force but by generosity and belonging; they would, in effect, be the ultimate individual. Ironically, the absolute singularity of the individual who belonged to no category was the foundation of the solitary regimes of incarceration that emerged in the nineteenth century.[129] Here, the opposite is envisioned: a free community in which all needs are met.

In such a community, poetry would also be different, 'since the distinction between public and private spheres, bound up as it is with the distinction between free and unfree activity, will have disappeared. Poetry might become both more intimate and more social all at once'.[130] Again, the social is imagined

---

[127] Édouard Glissant, *Poetics of Relation*, trans. Betsy Wing (Ann Arbor, MI: University of Michigan Press, [1997] 2010), 21.

[128] For Robert Lowell, the family 'allowed the subject to be seen in terms both Freudian and national-historical' and offered the possibility of recuperation. Javadizadeh, 'The Atlantic Ocean Breaking on Our Heads', 475–490 (483).

[129] Robin Evans, *The Fabrication of Virtue: English Prison Architecture, 1750–1840* (Cambridge: Cambridge University Press, 1982), 325.

[130] Jasper Bernes, Joshua Clover, and Juliana Spahr, 'Self-Abolition of the Poet, Part 2', *Jacket2*, https://jacket2.org/commentary/self-abolition-poet-part-2.

through and with the intimate: there's no getting rid of the latter. But it is the new world that will invent the new poetry, not vice versa. In the interim, the poet tinkers with grammar, seeding writing with possibilities for renewal that can be glimpsed in the riotous proliferation of nature and of the rebellious mass. This constellation – the singular individual not defined by identity categories or function, the community regulated by volition rather than violence, the poetics of intimacy and sociality – and the traces of its promise, as well as the obstacles to its achievement in the crises of the present, arise for Spahr in a context of radical anarchist politics. But they depend on a surprisingly faithful adherence to the traditional lyric.

Taking It: Settler Poetics

Spahr has said her formation as an experimental poet in college led her to be 'against lyric and confessionalism. The lines felt clear to me when I left SUNY Buffalo. And then I moved to Hawai'i and I realized that divide was a story that described certain poetries on the continent'.[131] This realisation is mapped in Spahr's prose work *The Transformation* (2007). Here, a polyamorous 'they' move to 'an island in the middle of the Pacific' (Hawai'i) to take up work in 'the complex' (a university). The book, which 'tells a barely truthful story of the years 1997-2001' (217), ends with a return to New York, where they are witnesses to September 11th and its aftermath (Spahr moved back to Hawai'i in July 2002). These events forced her to reconsider her complicities:

> I had to think about my intimacy with things I would rather not be intimate with even as (because?) I was very far away from all those things geographically. This feeling made lyric – with its attention to connection, with its dwelling on the beloved and on the afar – suddenly somewhat poignant, somewhat apt, even somewhat more useful than I usually find it. (*This Connection* 13)

Where Femi's poetry shows us the forced intimacy of the Black working-class subject with concrete, and Kapil reflects on the invasive intimacy foisted upon the guest by her prurient host, here connection and intimacy refer not to political movements or sexual relationships but to the binding of the American subject to militarised violence. At a distance from the US mainland, the subject is both 'far away' from the post-9/11 wars and very close to their colonial logic. In those conditions, lyric poetry – which Spahr, with her links to Language poetry, has

---

[131] Jos Charles, 'Interview with Juliana Spahr', *Entropy* (11 December 2015): www.entropymag .org/interview-with-juliana-spahr/. On the lyric nature of *Wolf*, see Raphael Kabo, '"Come Here, It Sang, Listen": Juliana Spahr's Commons Poetics in *That Winter the Wolf Came*', *Textual Practice* 35.7 (2021): 1195–1214.

previously eschewed – seems 'somewhat' useful for exploring intimate relations over distance.

The Transformation shows that Hawai'i was already prompting the poet's thinking about connections before 2001. There, 'they' are interpellated as 'haole', white people, akin to 'invasive species' of plants and birds such as 'the huehue haole that smothered shrubs, small trees, and the ground layer' or 'the scrubby kao haole that formed dense thickets and excluded all other plants ... Most of the birds they saw around them came from other places and took over' (31). But there are other creatures that arrive in Hawai'i embodying different forms of connectedness: 'the honeycreepers – the 'i'iwi and the 'apapane and the 'ākohekohe – who lived on the island before humans arrived yet no one knew how they got there because the birds were incapable of flying between the islands' (86); the land snails and koa and seeds and animals carried by winds. These species drift rather than invade, enriching ecosystems through the slowness of their integration. As such, plants and animals teach them about the 'bothness' of the place: violence and gentleness, theft and bounty. They want to be the land snail, but they are the huehue haole.

While they wish to 'escape from large systems, from limitations on relation' (33) into a non-hierarchical place within Hawai'i's ecology, they recognise that they are settlers whose historical presence depends upon those systems and limitations.[132] Spahr's book prods this aporia of privilege. They are anarcho-communists from working-class backgrounds in small rural towns who detest the state and its violence, and they are white American university professors teaching the literary tradition of an 'expansionist language' (English) in a colonised place who cannot alienate themselves from their status simply through conviction. *The Transformation* documents the discomfort that these irreconcilable differences produce within poetry and poetics, and the social and political life of their locality. Ironically, the book therefore exemplifies the tendency of haole poetry to be 'endlessly, almost absurdly, self-reflective' (93).

To manage their bad feelings, they develop strategies of accountability. These include rules for writing poems, reading groups to educate themselves about the island, and a commitment to 'take it' – to accept mockery and critiques from Kānaka Maoli. Taking it means submitting to a beating rather than acquiring or stealing. They also commit to 'take the accusative they into their bodies and let it change them' (48), to allow themselves to be infected by a realisation of who they really are as settlers imagined as a grammatical case. They learn from the

---

[132] On the history, ecology, and accession of Hawai'i to US statehood, see Dean Itsuji Saranillio, *Unsustainable Empire: Alternative Histories of Hawai'i Statehood* (Durham, NC: Duke University Press, 2018).

island that 'they were a they in the cruel inquisitive sense, in the sense of not being a part of us or we, in the sense of accusation, whether they wanted to be they or not' (21). Like the outsider who Femi's gatekeeper tries to keep out of the estate and/or the book, Spahr experiences being the object of aggressive address – becoming the 'you' that must 'take' the accusation, not the 'we' of indigenous Hawai'ian ecologies or traditions. They must learn to 'think with' this status, taking on the objectification that Femi and Kapil's Black and brown subjects have always already endured.

Faltering over Pronouns

At the heart of Spahr's poetics is a principle of relation that includes some unwanted connections (to colonisers, weapons dealers, climate destroyers, etc.) and is unable to fabricate other wanted connections (to the Kānaka Maoli we) except as the consequence of imperialist domination, while also longing for 'connection' to the full, abundant diversity of beings. *The Transformation* navigates this intricate relation between the domestic togetherness of 'them', the aesthetic togetherness of poetry, and the fragile political, social, and ecological togetherness from which they are excluded or which, by their presence, they destroy. They aren't part of the Hawai'ian 'we'; instead,

> They wanted to be they the way that humans might be they with a dog and a dog they with humans, intimately together yet with a limited vocabulary. They wanted to be they like blood cells are compelled to be a they. What they meant was that they were other than completely autonomous but they were not one thing with no edges, with no boundary lines. . . . They felt they could not allow themselves to be an us. (*Transformation* 207)

This is one of many examples in Spahr's work where relation is imagined through and with non-human others: the dog elicits a kind of being-with that is 'intimate' and tender, communicative but non-verbal, companionate and alleviating the need for linguistic exchange and likewise for poetry. Inhabiting the third person, giving up the privileges of the first and the conditions of address that can warmly invite or accusingly interpellate the second, 'they' also surrender something of their personhood. Émile Benveniste contends that 'the ordinary definition of the personal pronouns as containing the three terms I, you, and he, simply destroys the notion of "person." "Person" belongs only to I/you and is lacking in he'.[133] It is that lack of personhood that Spahr is grasping at in the compulsion 'to be a they'. They want to

---

[133] Émile Benveniste, *'The Nature of Pronouns'*, in *Problems in General Linguistics*, trans. Mary Elizabeth Meek (Coral Gables, FL: University of Miami Press, 1971), 217. Compare Claudia Rankine on the 'I': 'the pronoun barely holding the person together'. *Citizen: An American Lyric* (Minneapolis, MN: Graywolf, 2014), 71.

give up complex syntaxes, to adopt a sense of naturalised belonging that has no 'boundary lines' or, implicitly, borders – an unenclosed commons. A grammar fronted by 'they' within the unbounded form of prose expresses this edgelessness. The pronoun is not merely accusative, a sign of their willingness to 'take it', but an awkward pluralisation, an attempt to let others – not just one or two, but all the others – in:

> They agreed then to be enthralled with each other. They agreed to let the story they told about themselves as individuals be interrupted by others. They agreed to let their speech be filled with signs of each other and their enthrall-ment and their undoing. They agreed to falter over pronouns. They agreed to let them undo their speech and language. (*Transformation* 206)

But the language of the text is neither faltering nor undone; it is entirely clear prose. Interruptions by others are bracketed as indirect discourse. Judged by the doctrines of Language poetry, this work of auto-fiction offers less space for the reader's interruptions than Spahr's more explicitly poetic works; indeed, it at times verges on a kind of confessionalism.

Spahr's pronouns are not just aesthetic choices, but sites of political deliberation. They are one way for the poem to concentrate intimacies and publics, collectivities and singularities, to construct a commons that might also support the absolute specificity of personhood. 'I keep thinking pronouns all the time. Somehow pronouns have become the most loaded parts of language for me', Spahr told an interviewer in 2005.[134] Her early collection *Response* (1996) substitutes bracketed denominations such as '[gendered pronoun]' or '[generic plural pronoun]' for subjects.[135] In *Well Then There Now* (2011),

> I started with 'we' because I wanted to start with together. It is the idyll part of the poem. 'We' is humans and animals and plants. It is also knowledge when you are a child. You learn with and through others. And I wanted everyone to be there in the poem. I wanted 'we' to include those who read it. And then I wanted when I turn to 'I' to talk about how that moment of becoming individuals, becoming distinct and disconnected, is part of the problem. And I wanted more specifically to talk about my own complicity with this.[136]

The child's knowledge dissolves into a primal sympathy only half-remembered, as shades of the prison-house begin to close upon us. Individuation yields disconnection. This is a familiar Romantic idea about disenchantment and maturity.

---

[134] Michael Boyko, 'Brief Q&A with Juliana Spahr', *Tarpaulin Sky* (Summer 2005): www.tarpaulinsky.com/Summer05/Spahr/PRINT_Spahr_Q-n-A.html.

[135] Juliana Spahr, *Response* (Los Angeles, CA: Sun and Moon, 1996).

[136] Boyko, 'Brief Q&A', discussing *Well Then There Now* (San Francisco, CA: Black Sparrow, 2011).

And yet, like the Language poets who influenced her early practice, Spahr worries over the Romantic-aligned lyric 'I'. She identifies it as 'part of the problem', but also as a mechanism of accountability: it can 'stand up and take responsibility and be there in the poem', not 'hide in the "we."'[137] This accountable 'I' inhabits what Min Hyoung Song calls the 'revived lyric', which focuses on 'the space between a first-person speaker and a second-person addressee'; in that space, commonality is found and relation is posited that do not depend on some 'profound psychic interior'.[138] Spahr's writing expresses 'resistance and skepticism and doubt' about the proposition of artistic collaboration, and 'how it often seemed so focused on the I, I, I of their individual selves and their self-styled pseudo-heroic lifestyles, seemed so focused on the I, I, I of yet more autobiography, memoir, bourgeois individualist lyricism, and North American navel-gazing' (*Army of Lovers* 127–8). It is the reflective inwardness of the lyric 'I' that she eschews.[139] But that 'I' might also be construed as a site of exchange. Jonathan Culler argues that lyric can be 'freely' entered: 'Lyrics are poems made to be uttered by readers, who may come ritualistically to occupy the place of the lyric I.'[140] The quality of such freedom needs to be tested, as Walt Hunter has made clear, but this is also a tactical advantage: 'There is no separating the lyric "I" from its determination by economic status, by racial identity, by the cost of water or the price of oil or the ability to vote without having to present a voting I.D.'[141] Spahr's lyric is also constrained by a political scepticism about the real fungibility of that pronomial

---

[137] Boyko, 'Brief Q&A'.   [138] Min Hyoung Song, *Climate Lyricism*, 5.

[139] In a polemical rejection of such positions, Keston Sutherland argues that 'Artists and critics have been "rejecting" the "subjective" for hundreds of years, usually on whatever sketchy, skeletal, unexamined terms are nearest to hand. The antisubjectivism now being perpetuated by contemporary poets has no new features and it does not respond in any meaningful detail to its own historical moment.' Such a response would have to acknowledge, Sutherland argues, that 'Marx's account of the inhumanity of wage labour was precisely that it extinguishes the individual subject and reduces her to a mere quantity of "socially necessary labour power" and finally to *Gallerte*. Capital itself is the fundamental "antisubjective" force in the world and the pattern of all the others. Marxist revolutionary theory is about restoring the subject to society and abolishing the coercion that actually and in material reality desubjectivises workers.' 'Theses on Antisubjectivist Dogma', *A Fiery Flying Roule* (2013): https://afieryflying roule.tumblr.com/post/49378474736/keston-sutherland-theses-on-antisubjectivist. A related response would be to recognise the anti-subjective force of chattel slavery. As Fred Moten argues, Black people 'were not only assigned a value but a price, within a structure of vile politico-economic relations that are structured, in the first place, by the simultaneous imposition of individuation and the theft of the capacity to individuate. The individual person, that particular thing, obscures an undercommons to be claimed, which has so often been disavowed as blackness, which is its absolutely necessary and absolutely inexclusive historical form'. Fred Moten, *A Poetics of the Undercommons* (Butte: Sputnik & Fizzle, 2016), 29.

[140] Jonathan Culler, 'Lyric Words, Not Worlds', *Journal of Literary Theory* 11.1 (2017): 32–39 (35).

[141] Hunter, *Forms of a World*, 56.

subject. As her Hawai'i writing demonstrates, the rights or status of the first person are historically and culturally contingent, not universal. Culler's claim seems utopian; but a utopian imaginary, a being-with no longer impeded by force, is also partly what Spahr's poetics is after. And the rejection of the 'I' as merely navel-gazing also neglects the possibility, apparent across an abundance of lyric poems, that the poetic subject is what Alex Houen calls 'an impersona; one that relates selfhood and otherness as the result of imaginary projections, introjections, and identifications', rather than a straight-up authentic individual.[142]

Spahr also hesitates to use 'the dirty word of "we"', which 'assumes a false universal' and 'denies contradictions'. But, unlike the lyric 'I', she holds out hope that 'the "we" is also a great utopian pronoun and also a necessary one for various sorts of political action. And so I wanted to think about a wide "we" or a variant "we"'.[143] Bonnie Costello addresses this ambivalent, but hopeful, convocation of a first-person plurality in poetry, which 'often tries to bring into being a particular "we" that has been obstructed in history'. For Costello, the 'we' allows poets to expand metonymically beyond the small communities of its actual address, in a 'play of scale' that disavows claims to 'imperial authority or forced consensus'. It is non-coercive assemblage, a wishful expansionism without violence.[144] This is close to Spahr's practice, though she is more likely to acknowledge the need to fight.

Spahr's poetry doesn't idealise relation as such. Togetherness is riven with the violence of settler colonialism and capitalism, violence that is present even in gatherings of like-minded anarchists. As the 'Oakland Antagonists' wrote about Occupy Oakland, in which Spahr participated, 'The camp was a place of joy, laughter, and care, almost psychedelic in the confusion it provided to the senses. But mostly, it was a place that teetered on the edge of breakdown, a place in which none of the usual buffers and mediations that mask the daily violence of contemporary America were present.'[145] The camp could not eliminate capitalist dynamics of misogyny, homophobia, and racism. Spahr's poetry reflects this complexity, and rather than regarding moments like Occupy as temporary utopias, embraces the necessity of struggle within the collective. She writes 'about the fights we have had among ourselves over the last year': fights 'to get back to life, to refuse to die, to

---

[142] Alex Houen, 'On Inner Voice, Free Indirect Style, and Lyric', *Textual Practice* 35.6 (2021): 1037–1063 (1050).

[143] Bettridge, 'Conversation'. Here, Spahr echoes a now-standard Language poetry position, exemplified by Lyn Hejinian's critique of the 'coercive, epiphanic mode' of contemporary lyric poetry with its 'smug pretension to universality': Lyn Hejinian, 'The Rejection of Closure', *Poetry* (1983): www.poetryfoundation.org/articles/69401/the-rejection-of-closure.

[144] Bonnie Costello, 'The Plural of Us', *Jacket2* (January 2012): https://jacket2.org/article/plural-us.

[145] Some Oakland Antagonists, 'Rise and Fall'.

just feel. We fought because we became through fight. And because we don't agree and because we cared with an intensity' (*Wolf* 72). While fighting in Femi's book is a fearful possibility that leads to actual death, fighting in Spahr's work manifests both the violence of capitalism and resistance to it – even if it gets no further than throwing stones at cops. It is an expression of the wish not to die: it erupts from the tension of relation (not only among comrades, but between comrades and the state), cements and problematises togetherness. Revolutionary violence is necessary. Capitalism must be fought to be overcome. As Spahr and Clover wrote, 'This is how the misanthropocene ends. We go to war against it. My friends go to war against it. They run howling with joy and terror against it. I go with them.'[146]

In their guest editorship of the online magazine *Jacket2*, Spahr, Bernes, and Clover adopted a multivalent 'we' for their collective editorials, admitting they

> were perhaps a bit haphazard in our mixing-up of pronouns and points of view; after all, we have gone to jail for each other and bailed each other out and done each other's jobs and collaborated on many writings before and argued a lot with each too and then changed our minds as a result, and so it seemed to us pretty sensible. Sometimes the 'I' feels fraudulent also.[147]

The traditional authoritarian ring of the editorial 'we' is excused by an activist history of mutual aid – but both perspectives have a touch of fraud about them. Similarly, Spahr's pronouns attempt to expand the privileged 'I' and discover a syntax of solidarity with the ecological subject in its complex plurality. In Hawai'i, they begin to understand that 'the colonised lived under the mark of the plural, drowned in an anonymous collectivity that takes over their ability to talk about themselves as anything other than they' (*Transformation* 72). Transforming from 'I', the lyric subject, or 'we', the empowered subject of political enunciation or editorial *legerdemain*, into 'them', the absorbent and depersonalised object of action, indicates a desire to invert these historical relations. And yet, these pronouns often feel like placeholders, which cover a still-perceptible 'I' – thus exemplifying the limits of poetry to change actually existing relations.

Devotion to the Tradition of Eros

The problem of collectivity versus personhood that Spahr grapples with is not merely grammatical. It is lived, politically and erotically. Having rejected the couple form, 'We was undeniably a contested word for them. They often felt too

---

146 Joshua Clover and Juliana Spahr, *#Misanthropocene: 24 Theses* (2014): https://communeedi tions.files.wordpress.com/2014/08/misanthropocene_web_v2_final.pdf.

147 Jasper Bernes, Joshua Clover, and Juliana Spahr, 'Spring and All, Farewell to Jackets', *Jacket2* (2014): http://jacket2.org/commentary/spring-and-all-farewell-jackets.

large in it, too large because there were three of them instead of two' (40). As Spahr wrote on Bernadette Mayer's sonnets, 'their' multiplicity feels explosive: 'Once the lover merges into the beloved or once the lover's beloveds multiply or once the lover refuses gender's categories, what happens to desire's ricochet? When the atom turns unstable, one can make it into a bomb.'[148] Sex won't blow up a pipeline, of course; but the idea that nonconformist *jouissance* can produce an incendiary instability exemplifies Spahr's coupling of the pronominal with the erotic as ways of resisting capitalism and imagining its afterworlds.

Poetry, for Spahr, is just one way 'to think with others' (*Transformation* 115). The models for connection in her work mix militant action in the street with erotic intimacy in bed. Poetry is 'a philosophy of connection. Like a model of intimacy that was full of acquaintances and publics that recognized not only points of contact and mixing, but also relational difficulties, cultural and linguistic differences ... They felt writing in their body' (*Transformation* 188). Her poetry commits both to anti-capitalist struggle and to eros. It envisions sexual intimacy as a way of modulating between mass movements and the accountable I, scalar shifts that look also to welcome the creaturely world. She has argued that the reason 'poetry retains an aura of political usability in our culture is because it often mixes intimacy with politics': it can be an antidote to alienation. Political lyric proposes 'that we must approach our politics with as much devotion as we approach beloveds'. She jokes that 'The reason I like to hang out with poets is because they are devoted to the tradition of eros. To be at all interested in poetry means that at one point or another one had to declare an allegiance or an interest in how humans love things.'[149] Politics is strengthened by devotion, a commitment to love, that can be imagined primarily through the experience of eros; eros is one precursor of political action.

Spahr cites Anne Carson's argument that eros 'means want, lack, desire for that which is missing':[150] a 'hole' that is lyric's subject, a Lacanian absence and genital hole, constrained and mimicked by lyric form. For Spahr, lyric in specific political conditions can explore what might fill the hole, make it whole. As she concludes *An Army of Lovers*,

> we would sniff the herbs on our fingers while thinking and writing from our
> other skin, our other genders, our other holes, our other poses, our other
> others, all in adjacency, to the guns and the cars and the plot of land at the
> border between our cities, and to our lovers and our fleshy areas and our
> dildos, and to our leaking drill-holes and our leaking breasts and our overripe

[148] Spahr, 'Love Scattered', *Jacket2*, http://jacketmagazine.com/07/spahr-mayer.html.

[149] Bettridge, 'Conversation'.

[150] Spahr, 'Love Scattered', citing Anne Carson, *Eros the Bittersweet* (Champaign, IL: Dalkey Archive, 1998), 10–11.

insecurities, and to our stories, our biographies, our writing. And perhaps
from this we could then build a bottom-up, participatory structure of society
and culture, a two- and three- and more-way affair, about erect and sucking
participation. (121)

Society and culture emerge from the intimacy of the sexual, leaking, desiring
body.

But this imagined participatory structure ('bottom-up' in multiple senses) can
be thwarted by the enclosure of the body, the bed, the island, all 'small and
isolated' (*This Connection* 25), habits of privacy and privation that disaccustom
us to a commitment to the general. And this is partly why, as I wrote in the
Introduction, authors such as Sophie Lewis encourage us to imagine the abolition of the family, and Spahr finds potential in the expanded mutuality of
a polyamorous 'they'. Spahr notes that 'our world is small, contained within
1.4 to 2 square metres of surface area' (*This Connection* 23), no larger than the
volume contained by the skin. Even the desire 'to press against' others (33)
confronts the body's enclosure. 'They' are not edgeless, boundaryless, but that
is also what makes sexual pleasure possible. Like the small body, the small
influence of the self is imagined sexually:

> Beloveds, we do not know how to live our lives with any agency outside of
> our bed.

> It makes me angry that how we live in our bed – full of connected loving and
> full of isolated sleep and dreaming also – has no relevance to the rest of the
> world.

> How can the power of our combination of intimacy and isolation have so little
> power outside the space of our bed? (*This Connection* 25)

The speakers in Spahr's books know that they have 'so little power'. But as
Kapil's work suggests, intimacy and isolation *don't* have limited power beyond
the bedroom: they accommodate ideologies of property, scarcity, and protec-
tionism that expand right up to the border. While Kapil allegorises the politics of
states and migration as an allegorical couple or family, Spahr magnifies the
tenderness and viciousness of the bedroom to a planetary scale.

The bed is certainly not a utopian place. According to Piotr Gwiazda, it is
a site of 'alienation, passivity, and malaise': 'As Spahr well knows,
a withdrawal into one's bedroom in acceptance of the violence perpetrated on
one's behalf in itself amounts to an act of violence.'[151] Kapil might argue that
lying down in passivity constitutes a reclaiming of our sovereignty from the

---

[151] Piotr K. Gwiazda, *US Poetry in the Age of Empire, 1979–2012* (Basingstoke: Palgrave
Macmillan, 2014), 98, 101.

world that wants to force us constantly to move, work, shift. But Spahr asks a different question: how can poetry help to extend the way 'we live in our bed' to 'the rest of the world'? Especially when 'the power of our combination of intimacy and isolation', which is a lyric power, is contrasted with the useless-ness of poetry 'outside the space of our bed'? Spahr leans towards the power of rhetoric – to '*say* our bed is part of everyone else's bed' (my emphasis). But this is just saying. The declaration can imagine communising eros, but at best it calls attention to its discursiveness.[152]

Femi positions his subjects together in the softness of interiors as a way of guarding their vulnerability from the real violence of the state. But that violence is immediately present in Spahr's imagination: 'our bed is denied to others by an elaborate system of fences and passport-checking booths' (*This Connection* 30). The small room of the stanza, the whole world 'contracted' (as Donne wrote) into the lovers' bedroom, the lyric, are also enclosed by securitised borders and the violence of private property that makes the offer of communisation a thwarted wish.

Spahr imagines these erotic solidarities, but she also acknowledges their limits as tools to think or build a movement with. Overhearing another woman speak about her experience of the political moment around Occupy, Spahr writes: 'That moment. With. With. With. I am listening to her and I am with her.' But their togetherness is jaded; the woman speaks in the language of 'the private emotions of love and desire, the same emotions that are pillaged and packaged in popular music', a language 'given to her by multinational corpor-ations. A language of idealized family' (*Wolf* 73). This, at least, is something poetry can help with: detonating the language of idealised family, the commer-cialised rhetoric of love, and finding a different set of expressions that could accommodate the new feelings and realities of participating – however briefly – in riot and freedom. Nonetheless, the poet also confronts a challenge: how to categorise this being-with, this love, in ways that resist the gravitational pull of the language of family, or corporate sentimentality, or Marxist bromance?

Partly, Spahr's resistance is expressed as a hyperextension of eros beyond human beings, to the 'many possible loves' that make up the creaturely, animate, and inanimate worlds. 'I do not mean actual lovers. There are endless possible lovers. There are more than seven billion possible lovers most days. The categories of love, however, are multiple and yet also limited' (*Wolf* 73). Her speaker imagines fucking Chillicothe, Ohio,[153] or envisions 'Non-Revolution' as an erotic object in 'It's All Good, It's All Fucked' (*Wolf* 65–

---

[152] The phrase 'communise this eros' is from Rob Halpern, *Common Place* (Brooklyn, NY: Ugly Duckling Presse, 2015), 141.

[153] Juliana Spahr, *Well Then There Now* (Los Angeles, CA: Black Sparrow Press, 2011), 137.

77). But sex is not proposed as an a priori mode of non-dominating relatedness. As Siobhan Phillips notices about *Well Then There Now*,

> To put bed and table together, now, is to pollute both bedroom and boardroom with the power games of association. 'I wanted to end this piece with a scene of metaphoric group sex where all the participants were place names', Spahr writes in her penultimate section, 'but the minute I attempted to do this I got bogged down in questions of which places would penetrate and which places would be penetrated.' Love is a matrix of natural-cultural domination as much as a means of natural-cultural affiliation.[154]

Spahr's strategy is not to isolate love from politics or to propose poetry as the best means of imagining relations free of violence or inequality. Instead, in terms we recognise from Berlant's argument, she toggles between small- and large-scale relations to show how intimacy is permeated by state and ecological violence. She refuses the second part of the chiasmus: that state and ecological violence can be transfused with the life-giving properties of intimacy. 'Beloveds, I keep trying to speak of loving but all I speak about is acts of war and acts of war and acts of war' (*This Connection* 28):

> Beloveds, my desire is to hunker down and lie low, lie with yous in beds and bowers, lie with yous in resistance to the alone, lie with yous night after night.

> But the military-industrial complex enters our bed at night.

> . . . But I know there is no alone anymore here in the middle of the Pacific. (*This Connection* 63)

We are not alone, because we are together in bed – *we* refers to us lovers, but also to all Americans, all humans, and all creatures. In that synthesis, the military-industrial complex is also present. It is not content with presence. It colonises the bed and the intimacy, overpowering other forms of relation that might happen there.

Contamination and Doomed Connections

'When they wrote, they wrote as war machine. When they wrote, they wrote a ideological state apparatus. When they wrote, they wrote as military-industrial complex. The list went on and on' (*Transformation* 98). And lists do, in Spahr's work, go on and on. When they loved, they loved in the same way. The killing by the government 'moved into their apartment and lived with them. They were intimate and involved with it. It was an unwanted lover, one that was ruining the relationships they saw as real and yet they could not end this relationship they

---

[154] Siobhan Phillips, 'A Catalogue of Us with All: Juliana Spahr's *Well Then There Now*', *Los Angeles Review of Books* (2011): https://lareviewofbooks.org/article/a-catalogue-of-us-with-all-juliana-spahrs-well-then-there-now/.

had with the killing' (*Transformation* 193). Poetic personification allows a real abstraction to turn up in their bed. Their abusive relationship with the military-industrial complex provokes despair and contaminates intimacy; while the lovers sleep they are bedded down in 'the spinning earth, the gathering forces of some sort of destruction that is endless and happens over and over, each detail more horrific, each time more people hurt, each way worse and worse' (*This Connection* 36). Every morning, they awaken to the world as 'a series of isolated, burning fires' (*This Connection* 56), a series of apparently isolated incidents that, when consumed as news items, resist synthesis and trap us in a debilitating presentism, but when recorded in the poem or analysed through an anti-capitalist politics, reveal the systematising power of the state that 'they' wish to elude but cannot. Writing and loving are permeated by killing, and while there is no way to stop killing through writing or love, the making of lists at least allows them to attend to the bad kinds of relation that tie together the isolated, burning fires, and the good kinds that make the Niger delta teem with life.

I've written elsewhere about militarism and Latin erotic elegy: about how ancient Roman poets such as Ovid turned inward, away from imperial war towards the softness of heteroerotic desire. At the same time, their rejection of the Roman values of honour and heroic masculinity brought those struggles into the bedroom.[155] In *This Connection*, Spahr affiliates militarism and eros through a series of allusions to Sappho: 'some say thronging Warrior combat vehicles, some say foot soldiers, others call a fleet the most beautiful of sights the dark earth offers . . . / But I say it's whatever you love best' (45–6). (Sappho, her 'Sapphic rage', is an icon to whom Spahr frequently turns.) Repeating this refrain – whatever you love best is the most beautiful sight – is a way to extend the collective so that it might embrace 'the ones you love, those you've met and those you haven't': 'I say it again and again. / Again and again. / I try to keep saying it to keep making it happen' (47). Repetition takes on qualities of incantation. The beloveds are more beautiful than Warrior combat vehicles, are transubstantiated as weaponry. The list goes on and on. When 'I' stroke 'yours' body, 'I' stroke bombers and warships: the speaker is intimate with materiel, attending to it lovingly; they are also antagonised by the beloveds' militarised bodies.

The lovers' bed is contaminated by the military-industrial complex. More literally, the mother's milk is contaminated by industrial poison. Spahr's poem 'Tradition', from *Wolf*, concerns the many chemicals that the mother 'passes on' and 'hands over' along with nutrition, care, and love: 'a honeyed wine of flame

---

[155] Andrea Brady, *Poetry and Bondage: A History and Theory of Lyric Constraint* (Cambridge: Cambridge University Press, 2021), chap. 9.

retardants and fire preventing agents', 'a nectar of insulated pipes, and some industrial paints', 'a breast cup filled with sound insulation panels and imitation wood with a little nectar and sweetness' (*Wolf* 54). The infant grizzles,

> rebuking me, for my cakes of nuts and raisins
> are cakes of extraction of crude petroleum and natural gas,
> for my apples are filled with televisions and windshield wiper blades.

Behind the obsolete rhetorical bounty of cakes, apples, and honeyed wine, there is the dead matter of capitalism's waste products: impassive, cold, and irreducible. Steeped in the bounty of the mother's milk, there is capitalism's ability to destroy the habitable world.

Across Spahr's work, the list seems to be the only form capacious enough to hold all that is terrible about the world: product names gleaned from internet searches and raw information pile up indiscriminately, like the forever chemicals loading a body that will never be able to process them. But unlike the lists of 'vibrant matter' that Jane Bennett presents as a luminous ontology – random catalogues of 'vivid entities not entirely reducible to the contexts in which (human) subjects set them' – and as the grounds for a morality of 'decency', Spahr decorates her lists with self-consciously lyrical epithets to ironise consumption.[156] These commodities, adorned with love, mock reification and our inability to overcome it. Although the mother's transfer of chemicals in her milk is not deliberate, the child may blame her for the world it inherits at her breast. The child's 'song of rebuke' will have 'eighty-five company names in it. / It will have twenty-one chemical functions in it. / It will have ninety-seven products in it. / It will have two hundred trade names in it' (55). It will 'go on and on' (55) like a list, rotating 'through these names in all their combinations' (56). But something good and nurturing might also be transmitted along with the toxins through the parental body:

> I hold out my hand.
> I hand over
> and I pass on.
> Some call this mothering,
> this way I begin each day by holding out my hand and then all day long pass
>   on.
> Some call this caretaking,
> this way all day and all night long, I hold out my hand and take engine oil
>   additive into me and then I pass on this engine oil additive to this other
>   thing that once was me, this not really me.
> This soothing obligation
> This love. (53)

---

[156] Jane Bennett, *Vibrant Matter: A Political Ecology of Things* (Durham, NC: Duke University Press, 2010), 4–5.

Love is poisoned by capitalism, but the parent passes it on anyway, with critical knowledge of the cost of this donation and a wish for the empowerment of 'not really me', the child, by the complexity of what they receive: 'I say let wisdom be your anvil and knowledge your hammer' (56).

Spahr acknowledges the limits of political desire, construed as eros, which imagines relation only to that which is good. In reality, we incorporate much that we could never want:

> It was not all long lines of connection and utopia.
> It was a brackish stream and it went through the field beside our house.
> But we let into our hearts the brackish parts of it also.
> Some of it knowingly.
> We let in soda cans and we let in cigarette butts and we let in pink
> tampon applicators and we let in six pack of beer connectors
> and we let in various other pieces of plastic that would travel
> through the stream. (*Well Then* 130)

We let into our body and our streams and our poems the same morass of everything. But all the same, we loved it: 'we couldn't help this love because we arrived at the bank of the stream and began breathing and the stream was various and full of information and it changed our bodies' (*Well Then* 125). It's no use trying to keep all the information and plastic out. Capital's toxins are as inevitable as the organism's need for respiration.

'How lovely and how doomed this connection of everyone with lungs' (*This Connection* 10): Spahr repeatedly returns to breathing as an activity of connection and an expression of complicity. Breathing shows how 'we' become the 'they' who must take it, take lungfuls of dirty breath.

> This burning, this dirty air we breathe together, our dependence on this air, our inability to stop breathing, our desire to just get out of this world and yet there we are taking the burning of the world into our lungs every day where it rests inside us, haunting us, making us twitch and turn in our bed at night despite the comfort we take from each other's bodies. (*This Connection* 57)

In *The Transformation*, they breathe through a meditation exercise to overcome the anxiety induced by contemplating human destructiveness; they respire concrete and cars as well as grass and trees. It's deathly, but it calms them (133). After September 11th, breathing means ingesting poisonous chemicals and 'ghosts' – the material residues of buildings, objects, and people. This inspiration is not a form of healthy solidarity and togetherness, but poison. They have no choice. 'They tried to avoid breathing. It did not work. The air continued to enter their lungs like those operations that continued to be planned without their consent and despite their protest' (150).

Finally, in order to draw oxygen from this toxic air, they must expand and become 'monstrous in their heart ... That singular organ needed to be made bigger. They need to bring things inside of them that shouldn't be inside of them' (209). The impulse is almost shockingly twee: you must make your heart big enough to embrace the whole world! But Spahr tacks back to a biologised chant as she ends *The Transformation*, in which the heart is merely a set of valves pumping all the world's contents through itself: 'Pumped through the mitral valves the words of others. Pumped with the left ventricles the admission that they didn't have any real answers, only the hope that if they kept writing others might point them to answers' (214).

These erotic and tender currents, to return to Freud's hydrology, come together in Spahr's prose work, *An Army of Lovers*, co-written with David Buuck. In the title story, a breastfeeding parent works as an arms trader: 'when we fucked, ... my breasts would leak milk ... After we fucked, and usually before the ants figured out that there was milk in the bed, I would get up and sign another charter contract for the Il-18 with Centrafrican' (119). This leaking body, which sustains another, gives and takes pleasure, and sells weapons through complex international trading mechanisms, compiling both nurturing and destructive activities. The subject imagines building a new world: 'For motherhood and fucking exist as necessary paradigms of creation, ones where anyone can be an artist-lover and anyone can succeed. And through all of this I will continue to contribute, to bend and to leak, to adapt and mutate, adding yet more ingredients that we do not own to things that are beautiful, revolutionary, and irretrievable' (121).

This leaking maternal body, mutating and adding ingredients and passing them on, appears in two other short stories from the collection called 'The Side Effect', which propose non-verbal practices as ways of trying to acknowledge the paralysis of capitalist violence. In the second of these, the protagonist suffers from blisters that cause him increasing pain and sickness as he goes, every day, to a small studio to hold 'the pose of a person who was torturing someone or who was being tortured by someone' (*Army* 111). But the vagueness of the 'someones' who can either torture or be tortured and the inefficacy of his performances are related; the flow of torture, who takes and who gives, isn't typically reversible. His body is leaking – 'late capitalism leaked out of his face' (109), just as the military-industrial complex infiltrates the bed. His writing and performance achieve nothing:

> What he had meant to write was about his decision to do this project, to put his
> body into the position of particular others, that indexical other without whom
> no one can know one's own self. About his attempt to think of his life as part
> of a series of complex, passionate, antagonistic, and necessary relations to
> others who act and are acted upon. But it kept going wrong. (112)

Life, writing, and performance are practices of trying to put oneself in the place
of particular others: not through empathy, but through matter, sound waves, and
stress positions. These material and embodied practices, like sex or breastfeeding, might substantiate abstract ethical and political relations. But they don't
work. They induce 'reservations', 'mortifying and paralyzing shame', a sense of
'ineffectiveness', and despair 'about the limits of art done in isolation. About
the limits of art' (112). He gets sick; he makes soup.

This is the impasse that Spahr's work repeatedly confronts: the limits of art
and the need to keep going anyway. In the joyful climax of 'A Picturesque Story
about the Border Between Two Cities', a small plot of land becomes
a carnivalesque space where 'DJs spun and scratched the dented hubcaps of
half-exploded armed personnel carriers, the hillbilly armor attacked to sprawl-
ing networks of scrapped wiring and repurposed military hardware, improvised
exclamatory devices screeching into the general din and frenzy' (*Army* 31). In
this festival, torture and festivity are mixed; the site is, among many things, 'a
fake Baghdadi neighborhood staged for counterinsurgency training exercises',
an after-party, and 'an academic conference on politics and aesthetics' (33).
Festive collaboration, which absorbs into its anarchic and erotic energies all the
violence that maintains the state, is one way of overcoming the fact that poetry
doesn't matter. But it doesn't actually absorb; it mimics, and it is also a version
of carnival as safety-valve that is familiar from many critiques of Bakhtin. And
the danger, perhaps, with Spahr's oscillations between the bed and the everything, is that they risk being misread as an extension of lyric intimacy into
a corrective force that might overcome capitalist alienation through love and
parties. This is not Spahr's position, which recognises that revolution is the
means to overcome capitalism, and whose militance is grounded in the solidarities of the street; but it is a misreading made possible by her affection for lyric.

Lyric and Loss

An anti-capitalist poetic can offer alternative organisations and ecologies, kinds
of connections and personal and lyric intimacies that could include all the
animate and inanimate objects of the earth, revealing the 'intimate relationship
between salmons and humans, between humans and icebergs, between icebergs
and salmons' (*This Connection* 21). Spahr's wish for an erotic relation to the

billions of other lovers, and her thinking about the incorporation of toxins and other residues into the body, extends to encompass these more-than-human assemblages.[157] For example, in 'Transitory, Momentary', Spahr moves from geese to 'the many that are pulled from intimacies by oil's circulations', the oil and logistics workers and 'those on ships who spend fifty weeks circulating with the oil unable to talk to each other because of no shared language' (*Wolf* 14), and finally a line of activists passing bricks from hand to hand to construct a barricade. These different sociabilities all cluster in different ways around petrocapitalism: Brent crude is named after Brent geese, which are 'social, adaptable' (12); the activists stand in the 'shadow of love and a shadow of the burning of the oil fields' (15); all are at risk of losing their habitats to ecological disaster. But the poem, as Walt Hunter argues, is also a mediation on what can 'sustain a life': how to live under conditions of constant loss; how to keep singing there.[158]

The catastrophic consequences of our oil dependencies are examined in 'Dynamic Positioning', Spahr's documentary poem about the 2010 Deepwater Horizon disaster (*Wolf* 41–9). The poem brings to mind Wittgenstein's advice: 'Do not forget that a poem, although it is composed in the language of information, is not used in the language-game of giving information.' The poem contains technical information about the sequence of events leading to the oil spill, in concise language, without decoration or elaboration: 'At noon, a drill pipe goes in hole so as / To begin mud displacement' (45). That sequence unfolds across eight pages of unrhymed, roughly iambic couplets. At certain points it lapses into more recognisably poetic registers:

> I could go on and on here calling the
> New muses of innovation, common
>
> Vocabulary, that covers over the
> Elaborate simplicity of this (44)
>
> [. . .] I will tell the story of This Well (45)

But the lyric or authorial 'I' is largely absent, as is any other agency; the sentences are mostly in the passive voice. On the penultimate page, as the well explodes, the line breaks become more aggressive, erupting in the middle of words for nine couplets. After the disaster, the poem switches from action

---

[157] Heather Milne, 'Posthuman Assemblies: Ecopoetics and the Political Lyric in Juliana Spahr's *That Winter the Wolf Came*', *ISLE: Interdisciplinary Studies in Literature and Environment* 28.3 (Autumn 2021): 932–949.
[158] Hunter, *Forms of a World*, 115.

back to lists: the names of workers killed in the explosion, the names of supervisors, the names of CEOs of BP, Transocean, Halliburton, and the New York City Police Foundation. Although at its end the poem alludes to human agency, it refuses to drill down into the subjects' lives and deaths:

> I will not tell
> You their lives, their loves, their young children, their
>
> Relationship to oil. Our oil. The well
> Exploded. They then died. Some swam away. (49)

Here, Spahr uses the rhetorical figure of apophasis to introduce and foreswear the relations and liveliness of the workers. The most privileged forms of relation, between the dead and their grieving families, forms that a lyric poem might be expected to elegise, are suppressed. Instead, the dead are represented as components in a process that occurs seemingly amongst mechanised parts ('Blowout preventer open- // Ed, seawater then pumped down the drill / Pipe to displace the mud', 46). This work and the disaster is 'watched' from afar by other people whose roles incriminate them, and whose lives, loves, or young children are also irrelevant to the tragedy documented by the poem. The reader and the speaker participate in this 'watching' (49), but the poem has structured its release of information differently from the testimonies that would become available through lengthy litigation or from the sudden burst of oil pressure from below the ocean floor. 'Dynamic Positioning' uses metre and lineation to impose its slow, clear temporality on a disaster that led to colossal death across an entire ecosystem.

Following an ancient association between lyric and loss, Spahr imagines an art of song that 'can hold the oil wars and all that they mean and might yet mean within' (11), just as 'song holds loss' (12). That holding of loss – of defeat and disappearance, the future that disappears in the wake of defeat, and the living forms that disappear in every minute of the Anthropocene – preoccupies her throughout *Wolf*: it applies to the woman in a café regretting the passing of a riotous political moment (73), and to 'the depression that follows after the most mundane of uprisings is over' (76); it can be heard in 'a country song about abandonment' (77); it is the melancholia when 'it feels like it's over and it's not' or 'feels like it has just begun and it's over' (81). Spahr suggests that song holds loss through its form: it is built from stanzas and refrains that resemble the repetition of police clearing out a public space and the reformation of the crowd in their wake (11); 'the refrain is the moment when the singer makes it clear that they understand some-thing about what is being lost', even if that loss is 'minor' and personal, like 'the loss of tongue on clit or cock' (13). Questioning her impulse to write more formal verse – 'a poem about oil extraction in iambic pentameter' (20) such as 'Dynamic Positioning' – Spahr instead joins in the crowd's song:

> That winter we just rhymed and rhymed on. Together. Using words. Together. That winter everything suddenly written in our pentameters, our alexandrines, our heroic couplets, which was often an associational sentence-based quiet line, one indebted to lyric in which the we stood in for the beloved and yet there was almost never a description of this beloved . . . (60)

Form and prosody are ways of using words 'together', making verbal rhymes a mirror of the learning and being-with of people who waited under a tarp, together, for the arrival of a lone wolf in California, sadly named OR7, an animal 'alone' but 'looking for others' (59). Poetic convention is a coming-together, the histories of prosody and their overlooked assumptions places where we can sometimes 'just' do things that offer the solace of companionship beyond the present. We sing together, remembering all the traditional forms and the knowledge of the people who created them, resisting lyricisation's scarcity and liberal foundations.

Spahr's work repeatedly confronts the limits of art, the desire for revolution and for respite from anguish, the fear that relations (including lyric poetry) are too contingent or powerless to have any effect. She repeatedly articulates a relationship between poetry and politics that, like Kapil's lyric critique and critique of lyric, manages to be both sceptical (of the value of writing poems to create social change) and profoundly affirmative (of that value): 'We are not renouncing this desire that is poetry by recognizing that politics sometimes wants other things of us.'[159] Deploying repetition, refrain, and anaphora, Spahr's poems could, in Sonya Posmentier's terms, be described as 'ecological': they 'mimic or approximate organic forms and processes often associated with enclosure, preservation, self-sustainability, and internal relation, forms that can exceed their own boundaries, and that may in turn yield new models for social and ecological relation'.[160] Formal and pastoral respites are inadequate to face down the violent economic relations that are destroying the lifeworlds of humans and more-than-human others. How can we survive and thrive in these conditions? Spahr's poetry returns to the refrain of togetherness: 'We were with instead. But not just any old sort of with, but with each other in the hatred of capitalism. And if I was a poet of many centuries previous, I'd call that the sweetest wine of the beloved' (*Wolf* 69). Invoking the lyric beloved, she

---

[159] Stephen Voyce, '"Poetry and Other Antagonisms": An Interview with Commune Editions', *The Iowa Review* 47.1 (2017): 176–187 (177).

[160] Sonya Posmentier, *Cultivation and Catastrophe: The Lyric Ecology of Modern Black Literature* (Baltimore, MD: Johns Hopkins University Press, 2017), 4. Heather Milne makes a similar argument in 'Posthuman Assemblies'.

writes ardently about a different object: the crowd. And though history has so far suggested the crowd will not win, lyric poetry can picture its triumph and sing about our being-with in tenderness for each other and hatred of capitalism's.

4 Anne Boyer

This Element has so far considered the intimacies to be found despite racist and classist architectures of exclusion, in the protective embrace of the group, the allegorical dyad of the host and guest, and the erotic and carnivalesque connections among living beings across degraded ecosystems. The poems discussed in the previous sections locate themselves in material sites of struggle: the council estate, the border, the colony, the Occupy encampment. They also shift between these public sites and the intimacy of home as a related site of struggle, a space of erotic and familial tenderness that is both refuge from and expression of the violence of capitalism. The sickbed is another such site, where social and medical mechanisms for treating the individual person depend upon the supplement of privatised, waged and unwaged, caring labour. The legal apparatus that underpins work and the nuclear family inhibits the possibility of communised care, but that care happens anyway, and offers lessons for other forms of relation such as the crowd.

This section considers the work of Anne Boyer, a US poet, essayist, and visual artist whose experimental early books *Garments Against Women* (2015) and *A Handbook of Disappointed Fate* (2018) collected poetry and prose essays on themes of precarity, capitalism, gender, music, and digital alienation.[161] Boyer reached a wider audience and gained public recognition for her prose memoir *The Undying* (2019), which explored the 'violability and fragility' she experienced when diagnosed with cancer in August 2014.[162] Like Spahr's, Boyer's work is driven by an anti-capitalist ethic, a love of the crowd, and an attention to the way wounded bodies are open to the world's nutrients and poisons. Like Femi, she critiques state violence and describes the alienating effects of poverty and precarity. Like Kapil, she explores a politics and aesthetics of refusal: the sickbed is another place to lie down, in a passivity that resists the capitalist imperative to work. Boyer, like all these poets, also dreams of a condition beyond present crises, a future in which the commons can be reclaimed and the vulnerable cared for. This section outlines Boyer's

---

[161] Anne Boyer, *A Handbook of Disappointed Fate* (Brooklyn: Ugly Duckling Presse, 2018); Anne Boyer, *Garments against Women* (Boise, ID: Ahsahta Press, 2015).

[162] Anne Boyer, *The Undying: A Meditation on Modern Illness* (London: Penguin/Random House, 2019). Shoshana Olidort, 'Undying and Reparative Magic: A Conversation with Anne Boyer', *Poetry Foundation* (23 September 2019): www.poetryfoundation.org/harriet-books/2019/09/anne-boyer-undying-interview.

longstanding Marxist Feminist anti-capitalist poetics and its grounding in the lived experiences of poverty and precarity, which she connects to globalised supply chains through the feminised commodity of the garment. It explores her politics of refusal as the antecedent for the giant revolutionary 'no' that might overturn the disasters of private property, enclosure, and extraction, and burn up the existing order. These politics are tested in Boyer's prose writing on illness as a defamiliarising force that reveals the biases of the state towards conventional family structures, the necessity of communised care, and the need to imagine new spaces for collective recovery and mutual aid.

Anti-Capitalist Poetics

In her account of being stricken by and surviving, not just cancer but its treatment regimes and the assumptions of the state about caring labour, Boyer integrates contemporary American ways of being sick into larger critiques of state and capitalist violence that have preoccupied her poetry since the hectic, Flarf-inspired volume *The Romance of Happy Workers* (2008).[163] As she put it in her 2011 chapbook *My Common Heart*,

> Every poem until the revolution comes
> is only a list of questions
> so mourn for the poet
> who must mourn in their verse, their verse.[164]

Boyer shares with Spahr the perception that the poem in advance of the revolution is incomplete, a series of uncertainties that remind us of the conditionality of the future; it asks instead of proposing, and imagines rather than assuring. The poet grieves that incompletion, Non-Revolution's fickleness, Revolution's delayed appearance, and the inadequacy of her compulsive writing practice. She inhabits a sticky mid-point between critique and transformation. She is vaguely pathetic. Nevertheless, the pitiable poet keeps going, ashamed by lyric's self-expression, by the way that expression has taken over a world populated by digital selves, by being 'the dog who can never be happy because I am imagining the unhappiness of other dogs' (*Garments* 13). Boyer poses her mournful questions about precarity, capitalism, labour, and privacy, while anticipating the revolution that might unbreak our hearts.

Boyer has affirmed, 'I am definitely a communist. I believe that the world should be for the people and we should hold the world in common because it

---

[163] Anne Boyer, *The Romance of Happy Workers* (Minneapolis, MN: Coffee House Press, 2008). On Flarf and its relation to the workplace, see Jasper Bernes, *The Work of Art in the Age of Deindustrialisation* (Stanford, CA: Stanford University Press, 2017), 156–161.

[164] Anne Boyer, *My Common Heart* (Moorhead, MN: Spooky Girlfriend Press, 2011), unpaginated.

already is a common world. We shouldn't believe the lie of property ... It's labor that creates the world, and the people who think they have it have it wrongly.'[165] The commons as an archaic memory of shared resources and communality recurs regularly in her work. The commons are not just the spaces where the European peasantry coppiced wood and hunted for game, like St George's Hill, where Gerrard Winstanley and his comrades dug: they are a figure for 'what capitalism has always been committed to enclosing within its apparatus of accumulation', Julian Murphet argues. This plasticity – the commons as shared wealth, as whatever we lost – offers a 'nostalgic yet antagonistic class discourse of loss and resistance, [that] has come to stand for manifold social processes'.[166] Those processes include, for Murphet, the 'enclosures of language' (186) against which poetry militates. 'The poetic function, as a formal prophylactic, defends the linguistic commons against the automatisations of privatised speech, the encroachments of the capital-relation upon language', he writes (193). This is a good description of the position taken by Boyer's writing. Amidst capitalism's 'war against us and all we require to live', the poet is left mourning and asking questions, dreaming of lost commons of everything, including language.[167]

Capitalism's weapons in the war against life include the privatisation of property, the destruction of nature, exploitative work, commodification and globalisation, racialisation, and the nuclear family. Its war extends to the ends of the earth. Boyer's book *Garments Against Women* opens with an essay on 'The Animal Model of Inescapable Shock', which asks 'How is Capital not an infinite laboratory called "conditions"? And where is the edge of the electrified grid?' The prose poem depicts an animal dragged by 'a human who hurts her' onto an electrified grid where she is subjected to repeated shocks (1–2). By feminising the experimental object, Boyer 'particularises life under global capitalism' and shows how the experience of precarity is gendered within it, Walt Hunter argues. Boyer also demonstrates 'the impossibility of an external position', of a vantage from elsewhere than within capitalism's violence.[168] The text allegorises the regular shocks endured under capitalism, the shocks of urban life, and the shocks of the

---

[165] Callie Hitchcock, 'An Interview with Anne Boyer', *Culture* (1 October 2019): https://culture .org/an-interview-with-anne-boyer/.

[166] Daniel Eltringham, *Poetry & Commons: Postwar and Romantic Lyric in Times of Enclosure* (Liverpool: Liverpool University Press, 2022), 3. Julian Murphet, '"Wide as Targes Let Them Be," or, How a Poem Is a Barricade', in *Communism and Poetry: Writing against Capital*, ed. Ruth Jennison and Julian Murphet (Basingstoke: Palgrave Macmillan, 2019), 185–207 (185).

[167] Anne Boyer, 'The Heavy Air: Capitalism and Affronts to Common Sense', *Yale Review* (1 December 2020): https://yalereview.org/article/anne-boyer-capitalism-heavy-air.

[168] Hunter, *Forms of a World*, 40–1.

aesthetic analysed by Walter Benjamin, shock doctrine, and permacrisis. But it does so through a specific reference centred on the exploitation of animals: Martin Seligman's 1967 experiments, in which dogs were shocked by an electrified floor. In the first phase of the experiment, some dogs could escape by pressing a button; others could not. When placed on the floor, which was divided by a barrier into a shocking field and a non-shocking field in the second phase, only the dogs who had learned to escape in the first phase jumped the barrier. The dogs who originally were offered no form of escape experienced what Seligman called 'learned helplessness': an inability to help themselves, a passivity in the face of suffering. That is, a learned hopelessness. Seligman's theories were extrapolated as explanations for depression; but they also became the basis of torture protocols developed by the CIA for use in Abu Ghraib, Guantánamo Bay, and international black sites, though Seligman has disputed his contribution to the CIA's methods.[169] So the poem refers to a more specific violence than 'the deeply gendered shock conditions of contingent labour on a global scale' (Hunter 42), even though those conditions concern Boyer throughout the book.

The central theme of *Garments* is not US necropolitics, however, but private property ('it has altogether ceased to be practical to own things in the months of January and August. Strange thing to insist that we own', 17) and the violence by which it is maintained ('On the time I saw a homeless man murdered for shoplifting / On whether it is better to want nothing or steal everything', 47). Boyer's parody of gendered consumerism, 'A Woman Shopping', laments 'the incompatibility of life forces and living beings (all? many?) who the present arrangement of the world has made to live without access to life's fullness, as all that is life is always being transformed into instruments not of love, but of profit' (48). Accessing life's fullness would not entail more consumption, but less: maybe even a strike against shopping, a collective revolt against the 'feminised marketplace' (48). This is what Mariarosa Dalla Costa and Selma James imagine when they argue that 'Women do not make the home the centre of consumption. The process of consumption is integral to the production of labour power, and if women refused to do the shopping (that is, to spend), this would be strike action.'[170] But, as with threats by the Wages for Housework movement to withdraw unwaged reproductive labour, this strike against consumerism is

---

[169] See Tamsin Shaw, 'The Psychologists Take Power', *New York Review of Books* (February 2016): www.nybooks.com/articles/2016/02/25/the-psychologists-take-power/ and '"Learned Helplessness" & Torture: An Exchange', Martin Seligman, reply by Tamsin Shaw, in *New York Review of Books* (April 2016): www.nybooks.com/articles/2016/04/21/learned-help lessness-torture-an-exchange/.

[170] Mariarosa Dalla Costa and Selma James, *The Power of Women and the Subversion of the Community* (London: Falling Wall Press, 1972), 44–5.

easier to imagine than enact. Opting out of the economics of fast fashion by making your own clothes, for example, might align you with the wholesome world of internet moms and crafters with an abundance of time on their hands, rather than enacting solidarity with feminised and globalised labour. 'Sewing' places the speaker's amateurish efforts to make clothing for herself and her daughter within the latter framework. Nonetheless, Lyndsay Turner has argued that the poem's 'condition of paralyzing embrace resembles what Bruce Robbins has called the "sweatshop sublime," or the perception that one's daily existence is tied into a whole web of precarious existences'.[171] Turner critiques how these garment workers 'appear to [Boyer] as they do to a majority of Western consumers, almost invisible', 'acknowledged as present, but rendered distant and mediated through the internet, through literature, and through multiple steps of backwards mathematical calculation' (132–3). The electrified grid is edgeless, but not everyone is subjected to the same level of shock; the hopelessness induced in people positioned on it depends on the absence of an escape button. This could be wealth, but also sometimes includes poetry, and the solidarity of comrades.

In recent essays, Boyer considers how the pandemic, Occupy, and anti-Black police violence have intensified the struggle against the existing order and the need for mutual aid. She is repulsed by the fetishism of commodities and the fungibility of human life: a world in which 'things become like people and appear to take on a life – even rights – of their own', while 'people are made to be as things in that they are fractured, injured, used up, wasted, exploited, branded, self-exploited, self-branded, tossed out'.[172] In early experiments informed by Cartesian philosophy, animals were perceived not to feel pain: 'the cry of a beaten dog was no more evidence of the brute's suffering than was the sound of an organ proof that the instrument felt pain when struck', as Keith Thomas summarises it.[173] Descartes objectified animals as mere automata, machines incapable of meaningful sensation. In Boyer's Marxist analysis, humans are now also treated like things, machines condemned to 'be overwhelmed with feeling'. Lyric as a genre associated with feeling, whose apostrophes imagine a way of relating to inanimate things as objects of address, might be useful for navigating this reality.

But lyric's usefulness is limited. Boyer rages against 'information-damaged life', the antagonisms of the internet, the theft of our time, data and feelings by

---

[171] Lindsay Turner, 'Writing/Not Writing: Anne Boyer, Paralipsis, and Literary Work', *ASAP Journal* 3.1 (January 2018): 121–142 (123).

[172] Goldstein, 'Find Something to Hide'.

[173] Keith Thomas, *Man and the Natural World: Changing Attitudes in England 1500–1800* (London: Penguin, 1983), 33.

capitalism.[174] The digital was once a commons, a rhizomic and laterally organised zone of piracy and deletion, of 'turning property into nonproperty, of liberating the common'; now it is a bottomless pit of doom scrolling and manipulation.[175] The commons, yet again, has been enclosed. Online, everyone is a degraded lyric poet, fashioning sensitive subjectivities from the carefully cropped accidents of daily life, taking momentary positions, coping with form, eliciting relations of intimacy with communities of like-minded readers who eavesdrop on supposedly authentic confessions spoken in the solitary cell of the device as if no one is listening. And, for the most part, no one is. Poetry, whose techniques have developed complex capacities for representing and denaturing feeling, could be part of the resistance to the reification of subjectivity in the digital age. Its complexities should be antithetical to the reduction of thinking to the 'take'. But poetry is now, Boyer argues,

> as searchable and immaterial as any other information. As it always has, poetry experiments in fashionable confusions, excels in the popular substitutive fantasies of its time, mistakes self-expression for sovereignty. But in making the world blurry, distressing, and forgettable, poetry now has near limitless competition … Deprived of posterity, poetry softly imitates the information that always is claiming to be us. Then information, like to like, devours it.[176]

A poem like Spahr's 'Dynamic Positioning', I argued, perturbs the language-game of giving information through the irreducibility of its prosody, using iambic pentameter and the antagonisms of the line break to offer a new common ground of understanding in the murk of the Deepwater Horizon disaster. This is not poetry imitating information, but poetry using its technical specificities and histories to call attention to the damage entailed in mimesis and data-exchange. But Boyer's fear – that poetry risks becoming submerged in the vast ocean of reporting from plangent subjectivities, just a faltering node within a strangulated attention economy – would be more persuasive if it included some specification about what poetry is, or could be: what distinguishes it from other discourses. If poetry, that is to say lyric, is just about being a subject condemned to have feelings, then it will be devoured. But maybe it is more complicated than that.

---

[174] Anne Boyer, 'The Same, All-Coordinating Light', *Mirabilary Substack* (20 December 2019): https://anneboyer.substack.com/p/the-same-all-coordinating-light.

[175] Anne Boyer, 'The Earthly Shadow of the Cloud', *Mirabilary Substack* (30 March 2021): https://anneboyer.substack.com/p/the-earthly-shadow-of-the-cloud.

[176] 'Click-Bait Thanatos', *Handbook*, 115.

Poor Life

Boyer criticises writers who fail to acknowledge the reality that 'in order to live, the vast majority of people have to sell the hours of their lives at work'. Although this fact organises almost all human activity, 'much of the most lauded literature locks this up like a secret inside itself'.[177] This 'lauded literature', which cordons off its attention to matters of personal experience, focuses on 'feelings, self-identification, self-interest, self-fulfilment, self-determination', as if 'humans were made from the inside out, instead of the outside in, and that the only relation to objects we had was our curation of them'. This canon is distinct from the poetry that seeks to imitate information. While the former is too small, the latter is too big. One cultivates an inwardness of crystallised verities, the other is lost in a blizzard of ephemera. Neither offers a useful analytic. Reality is either groomed or elided; many important things are left out as unpoetic.

As Boyer writes in *Garments*, 'I feel like I read some, but still there are so many things of such importance about which I have never found a book' (5). She marvels that 'I am not sure that beyond the work of radical poets, I've ever seen much mention in literature that a car requires gas, that the gas requires the oil industry, the oil industry requires imperialist war, etc.'[178] Feeling displaces critique of the material conditions that produce the senti-mental subject. By contrast, Boyer's own writing tries to acknowledge that a car needs petrol, which implicates the car and its owner in capitalist and imperialist violence, and that petrol costs money, without which a particular person, or car, might break down. That is to say, her work is lyric in that it ties its universalising anti-capitalist poetics to individual experiences of poverty and struggle. She has said that she is a feminist poet 'because I write for one reason: the landlords insisted we had heat when the tenants knew we were freezing. It was sixteen degrees, and we tried everything to get warm like burning the signs the landlords had written for us: "the heat is on".'[179] Feminism takes a theoretical and practical position on tenancy and private property; but it is expressed as a moment of writing in and about the home, about her and her daughter and the other tenants' struggle with their actual landlord. That sign recurs in *Garments Against Women*, where the tenants respond with more writing: 'I decided I would be a poet so that I could complain publicly of this' (57). A lyric poet integrates structural critique

---

[177] Goldstein, 'Find Something to Hide'.   [178] Ibid.
[179] Anne Boyer, 'On Being a Feminist Poet', *Delirious Hem* blog (4 May 2009): http://delir ioushem.blogspot.com/2009/04/by-anne-boyer.html.

with personal experience. Her signs are read by more people than just the tenants of the Kingman building.

Experiences of poverty and precarity inform all of Boyer's writing. In *My Common Heart*, she laments, 'I'm full of big promises. I'm tired. I work three jobs. I am unceasing but also I am so totally ceasing and sometimes almost ceased.'[180] Like feminism and the heating, poverty is both an abstract category susceptible to a Marxist analysis, and a specific, material, enumerated, embodied experience that lyric poetry is made to register:

> It was a time of many car troubles, so I waited for tow trucks and saw a squirrel with a marble in her mouth. It was a time of many money troubles, so I wrote about money or wanted to. .... What was I, poor? I spent seventy-three cents on a cookie for my daughter. I got a fifty-dollar Wal-Mart gift card in the mail. I sold a painting of a lamb for three hundred and eighty-five dollars. (*Garments* 69)

This is not traditional lyric. It's not lineated, for a start. It withdraws into itself not in pursuit of universality but because of its preoccupation with money troubles and the need to secure even the most basic reproduction of life. No one here has time to dwell on their feelings. Instead, they are preoccupied with necessary calculations. The speaker in 'Sewing' makes her own garments not just for the satisfaction of crafting, but because:

> I make anywhere from 10 to 15 dollars an hour at any of my three jobs. A garment from Target or Forever 21 costs 10 to 30 dollars. A garment from a thrift store costs somewhere between 4 and 10 dollars. A garment at a garage sale costs 1 to 5 dollars. A garment from a department store costs 30 to 500 dollars. All of these have been made, for the most part, from hours of women and children's lives. Now I give the hours of my life I don't sell to my employers to the garments. (*Garments* 29)

Working multiple jobs for close to minimum wage, the speaker tracks Marx's famous M-C-M' equation, using money's abstract equivalences to convert her labour into a fast-fashion item, in a calculus of solidarity that aligns her impoverishment with the worker who produced the garment: anywhere from one to three hours of her life to buy the thing that was produced by hours of the lives of women and children garment workers. Her sewing connects her to the class of other feminised workers who have nothing to sell but their labour power. As such, 'it is probably more meaningful to sew a dress than to write a poem' (29), which offers no such equivalences, or only the ones between poetry and property ownership.

---

[180] 'Two Versions of the Song', *My Common Heart*.

Capitalist conditions produce suffering, even if there is not time, when all time is stolen as waged labour, to express that. Boyer has said:

> I have lived the shit bottom of the barrel life for more years than I have ever lived any other kind, most of it my own fault, crying in parking lots outside the call centers crying in break rooms crying in cubicles and restaurant kitchens crying without jobs and also crying with them, crying for love and also against it and also because of it and without it.[181]

Another poem in *Garments* describes a sad outing to the mall to buy new shoes for her daughter. The child wants $44 shoes and mourns the necessity of accepting a cheaper alternative. When the mother wants to cry, the daughter says, 'you have had many years of dreams and realities to learn from so there is no excuse for you to cry' before asking, 'do you have enough dreams?' (38). The daughter is being inducted into the trauma of private property and inequality, her dream of consumerism dashed by the reality of poverty. It's possible, if difficult, to calculate whether you have enough money, or things, in order to reproduce yourself and make yourself ready to return to work. But it's less possible to calculate if you have 'enough' dreams to avoid a learned hopelessness: a hopelessness that might also be learned, or reproduced, by the daughter, who is still young enough to imagine 'a world without things', in which people would 'make things with trees and dirt' (58), refusing capitalism's logic. But the poem can incorporate both the reality and the feeling –the mother's experienced grief and the daughter's dream.

Just Say No

Dorothy Wang asks, 'Can "flatness" of tone be a form of poetic and political rebellion? An insurrection from within. The poem's refusing to rise to the occasion. *Nothing to go apeshit for*'.[182] Like Spahr and Kapil, Boyer adopts a flat tone. Her writing tends to understate feeling, to depict it dispassionately, rejecting lyric's affective intensities with statements of fact and enumerations whose coolness belies the urgency of survival that depend on those calculations. Working in units that Ron Silliman names 'the new sentence',[183] she emphasises time and experience not as sentimental fodder for writing but as units of capitalist production, and imagines the end of such quantifications: 'No more duration as unit of infliction – no work hours, prison sentences, deadly prognoses. No more believing in centuries,

---

[181] Anne Boyer, 'Two', *Mirabilary Substack* (30 May 2018): https://anneboyer.substack.com/p/two.

[182] Wang, 'Speculative Notes on Bhanu Kapil', 78–91 (83).

[183] Ron Silliman, *The New Sentence* (New York, NY: Roof Books, 1987), 63–93.

generations, war as what begins and ends, the rude periodizations of historians on the payroll. .... No one on earth should have to wish away his or her time on it' ('Heavy Air').

This prayer combines the analeptic and proleptic attunement that Boyer says must remain a list of questions until the revolution comes. Its resounding 'no' is a consistent theme in Boyer's work, which resolutely refuses things as they exist, or celebrates the capacity of others to refuse. The poems reject the rationalised time of alienated labour (including reproductive labour), mass incarceration, and war, reaching instead towards a time that can be enjoyed personally and communally. It is difficult to wait, but in the meanwhile, the capacity for refusal sustains us: 'Can a fucked up world make a non-fucked up literature? Probably not. Can we give up trying? No. Why not? Because of the very capacity of a "no," of the soul itself, which humans possess together, contains within it the ingredient of the possible, including a possible literature and a possible world.'[184] Like Kapil's figures who lie down, exhibiting a radical passivity that reclaims individual sovereignty at the moment of extinction, every person can exercise their capacious 'no' and find in it the seeds of the possible.

Refusals are enacted in many of Boyer's poems. *Ma Vie en Bling: A Memoir* (published as a chapbook in 2008 and included in *Garments*) includes a fragment of resistance in the grip of defeat, which I picture as a revolutionary woman on a scaffold, refusing to climb to her death: 'I will tell the story like this: it appears that she refused the ladder, but in truth she refused the rope' (81). The essay 'No' is a panegyric to 'people who just didn't' (*Handbook* 9):

> Some days my only certain *we* is this certain *we* that didn't, that wouldn't, whose bodies or spirits wouldn't go along ... And still we ghost, and no-show, and in the enigma of refusal, we find that we endogenously produce our own capacity to even try, grow sick and depressed and motionless under all the merciless and circulatory conditions of all the capitalist *yes* and just can't, even if we thought we really wanted to. (10–11)

Boyer dilates specifically on poetry as 'sometimes a *no*. Its relative silence is the negative's underhanded form of singing' (11). Through its 'transpositions', radical imaginaries and reversals of what exists, poetry 'can protect a potential yes' (16), and provide a ground where both refusal and re-ordering are legible and therefore social. 'No' 'presides over the logic of my art' (13), she says, and through the poetic and the political no, the lyric 'I' can join the communal 'we' who throughout history have refused: those who 'turned away, escape to the desert, lived in barrels, burned down their own houses,

---

[184] Goldstein, 'Find Something to Hide'.

killed their rapists, pushed away dinner, meditated into the light' (9). Unlike
Nietzsche's *amor fati* as a complete and embodied 'yes' addressed to all aspects
of existence, even that which is 'forbidden or diminished or degraded', Boyer's
'no' serves as a token of 'a deeper mystery, which is what we can truly love,
what we truly want to say yes to'.[185]

'I would rather write nothing at all than propagandize for the world as is'
(*Undying* 116). Boyer's poetry dances along this paradox, in which the refusal
to write would be a more committed practice than a writing that comes to terms
with what is. 'Not Writing' and 'What is Not Writing' in *Garments* reflect on the
reproductive and other forms of labour that displace writing. The book was
written around 2010, when Boyer and her daughter were dealing with

> the kind of poverty in which you are always getting sick from stress and
> overwork and shitty food then having no insurance or money or time to treat
> the problems caused by having no insurance or money or time. I began to believe
> that it was the extra burden I put on myself to be a writer that was making me sick
> and that we would be a lot happier and healthier if I could give it up.[186]

Sickness is obviously linked to poverty, but writing, which might be idealised as
an alternative to capitalism's punishing economies and the pain of being a thing
condemned to feel, can make poverty feel worse. Poverty necessitates the
refusal of poetry, or rather prioritises direct pragmatic action over the non-
productive use of time dedicated to the crafting of the text. In 'Kansas City',
Boyer tells a life story about realising she couldn't be a poet: 'I was soon inside
whatever was not a poem, working in the shelters and community centres of
Kansas City and thinking the only possible life was a life of politics, and the
only possible politics was a politics for women and children and the poor'
(*Handbook* 35–6). This political work is to share the space of the poor which is
'not a poem'; it is an act of refusal grounded in solidarity.

For a poor person, writing is a paradoxical activity. It evades capture by
capitalist logic, until it doesn't; it is unwaged, until it becomes an aspect of the
precarious, and later secure, day job; it seems like a relief from work and
sickness, or it contributes to them; it is an avenue to prestige and advancement,
whether or not these things are wanted when they come from systems that
mostly produce poverty; it is against money and (sometimes) it makes money.
Boyer admits that

---

[185] Hitchcock, 'An Interview'.

[186] Amy King, '"Literature Is against Us": In Conversation with Anne Boyer', *Poetry Foundation*
(30 August 2015): www.poetryfoundation.org/harriet-books/2015/08/literature-is-against-us-
in-conversation-with-anne-boyer.

I've had a difficult time believing I could share my writing, interested in wanting nothing and in the walled complexities of gardens and libraries, feeling exhausted, semi-sick, and lost. I did not know how the lost could write, or what we could say, or if we should say anything, until walking down the stairs from the attic, I had a revelation: *how the lost can write is for the lost.* And so we who draw angels with our eyes closed should not be bereft of our own literature, even as making it is a fragile activity, having only an embarrassed relation to capitalism's dire opinionating from platforms of carbon-economies and blood.[187]

As Adorno has argued,

> poetic subjectivity is itself indebted to privilege: the pressures of the struggle for survival allow only a few human beings to grasp the universal through immersion in the self or to develop as autonomous subjects capable of freely expressing themselves. The others, however, those who not only stand alienated, as though they were objects, facing the disconcerted poetic subject but who have also literally been degraded to objects of history, have the same right, or a greater right, to grope for the sounds in which sufferings and dreams are welded.[188]

Boyer's work recognises those privileges, but also reflects on their burdens. Struggling to pull oneself from objecthood to subjectivity, groping for form and time, can be impossible, lonely work. But she does it not by grasping at individual autonomy. Instead, she affirms her membership in the collectivity of the lost, writing for and with them.

The Dream That Revolution Can Live

Writing the book of the lost, the book of the collective, refutes the no that is poverty with the no of solidarity. The biggest, most miraculous no that can be imagined is revolution. For Boyer, this refusal is anticipated in the small no's that prepare the ground for cataclysmic change. Boyer promises that 'the force that annihilates the changing nature of the universe, the always becoming that constitutes life, won't be capitalism, which will not last forever': instead, the overthrow of existing conditions could show us the edge of the electrified grid.[189] Meanwhile, even in such gestures as sharing a recipe for cake for those who own only one small pan, Boyer's work proposes other ways to resist oppression in the present. She suggests:

---

[187] Anne Boyer, 'Each Homer of Nought', *Mirabilary Substack* (5 July 2021): https://anne boyer.substack.com/p/each-homer-of-nought.

[188] Adorno, 'On Lyric Poetry and Society', 37–54 (45).

[189] Anne Boyer, 'Something Divine Was Promised and It Melted Away in the Mouth', *Mirabilary Substack* (2 September 2020): https://anneboyer.substack.com/p/something-divine-was-prom ised-and.

> Put your body in minor places unwelcome to your body. You may start with
> places rented or leased to you or places in which you have a kind of tentative
> and half-access or right. Ten minutes under your own bed in your rental home
> or apartment. Then, also, fifty minutes sitting quietly on the strip at the end of
> the yard, the easement owned by the city and on which the city won't let you
> plant rosemary or carrots. ('Preoccupation', *My Common Heart*)

Such brief acts of resistance are 'minor' disturbances of an order that works to
extinguish pleasure for poor people. But they are good practice. Here again, she
stresses quantities, instructions, a flat style of very direct address, emphasising
not the lyric feeling of resistance but the action that might engender it. The
pathos is in the small details: the small, nourishing plants you are not allowed to
grow; and your refusal to accept their prohibition, or the hostility to your own
body. These strategies recall the guest's small gestures in Kapil's work, as well
as the narrow precincts in which the guest was able to feel welcome.

In *My Common Heart*, Boyer speaks from a position of hopefulness: that
revolution, like a newborn child, can live; that the poet's lyric heart can be
contemplated and then overlooked in 'a season of revolution', when appears
'To my / great relief – / the world'. In this text, the gestures are big. 'ALL OF
A SUDDEN THE CITY ON FIRE' shows us a speaker basking in the glow of its
burning, knowing that the vulnerable – the city's animals, its women and children – are unscathed by the conflagration razing the city in order to build it anew.
The poet joins in not as an unacknowledged legislator but as 'an arsonist',

> receiving no pay for this,
> I volunteer as a soft minister
>   of burning up
> the known and unknown
>
> brothels, daycares and call centers
> living rooms, city blocks
> the women and children
>   glowing finally
>   like animals
> more visible than nature!
> I knew it!
> I am that woman! I have a child!
>
> the once empty factories are busy now
> with unions of flame
> cooperative and mutual! (*My Common Heart*, np)

Boyer's ecstatic exclamations recall Spahr's fantasy of taking the hand of
Revolution 'and be[ing] led to whatever room when it comes because oh my
god, the body of Revolution is something magnificent. But I also know that at

that moment I will know the meaning of it's all fucked so hard' (*Wolf* 71). Boyer's fantasy of a city good for burning doesn't tarry with anticipation of how 'fucked' everything will be when it happens. The flames selectively consume what's bad – spaces of feminised labour such as the brothel, childcare, call centre, and factories – and somehow remake the traditional forms of worker solidarity, such as the cooperative, mutual aid society, and trade union. The authorities are in flight. The poetic imagination rewrites history on the scorched earth of capitalism's structures.

Boyer suggests that the preparatory work for this fantastic conflagration is already underway. In 'The Crowd' (*My Common Heart*), Boyer pays tribute to the crowd's radical and interdependent nature, which 'often starts with women together conspiring', 'is never neoliberal in its desires' and is 'the remedy for the state'. Writing more recently about Occupy Kansas City, Boyer describes such a crowd in action, 'always gathering and falling apart, clustering and scattered . . . When I leave the occupied space of the city into the ordinary space of the city, the ordinary space has ceased to feel real . . . My feeling for the occupation is almost exactly like love, vulnerable and half-mad, but I am handing my heart not to another human but to an unfixed, circulating crowd' ('Kansas City', *Handbook* 30–1). The new history imagined in 'ALL OF A SUDDEN' is anticipated in such moments. The speaker exchanges her heart not within the exclusive relation of the couple form but with what Spahr called 'not really me', the crowd whose energies gather and disperse in waves that resist stasis or capture.

Like Femi's love for the endz, or Spahr's love for Non-Revolution and the occupation, Boyer's love for the crowd looks for its analogue to erotic love, an exchange of hearts. But it expands to become something else. In 'Erotology', Boyer moves from the desire for 'the one-ness of this one person' to a recognition that 'You hold a face in your eyes a lot and say "I am a citizen of longing for that one person," but what you really mean is that you are a citizen of longing for the world' (*Handbook* 85). Erotic love is a pedagogy of desire for the other that expands beyond the personal. The crowd can be the space where that collective longing is realised, and for the fulfilment of needs that are usually privatised. It provides a sentimental space for the flourishing of communal life: 'These are the commons: "my heart." This is the common: "my heart"' ('Who Are All These People What Is All This Money', *My Common Heart*). This elevation of the heart is very different from its exposure in Kapil's book. Here, the heart becomes a collective resource, safely made public, rather than a figment of privatised feeling and lyric interiority that is susceptible to a devouring predator.

The crowd is sustaining; an individual, alone, 'can do almost nothing. She cannot make children or be a poet alone. . . . If she dies alone she is less than dead' ('The Crowd', *My Common Heart*). These are ancient claims about solitude, which, according to Aristotle and Sir Francis Bacon, only a wild animal or a god could endure. Boyer proposes a thought experiment: stand in a large stadium and imagine that each one of the people you see is a baby. 'Each grown person, each grown human being, represents ambulatory, irrefutable evidence that we know how to take care of one another and that we have something more in us besides the narrow, selfish, competitive world that capitalism creates for us.'[190] Each person, taken together, also signifies the possible worlds that we could organise for our flourishing. As she repeatedly insists, we exist only through and because of the collective labour of others:

> No one is ever born alone, and no one is in a bigger crowd whoever has joined the company of the dead, and no one in between birth and death is ever anything but a person in a world full of other people, full of animals and objects, full of things and their relations, full of processes and histories and types of weather.[191]

Such imaginings lead to a 'philosophy of radical care'; 'an ethics and metaphysics and poetics of the most passionate attachments like that of a mother for her child', without sentimentalising or prioritising reproduction as a gendered activity: a radical tenderness.

Sickness as Knowledge

Boyer's tender attention to ameliorating the experiences of poverty and precarity, particularly as they are gendered, and to imagining the ongoing possibility of overthrowing capitalism while committing to offer solidarity, mutual aid, radical care and recognition of the interdependence of all life, come together in *The Undying*. In this book, Boyer turns from the avant-garde poetic strategies deployed in her earlier work to short passages of clear, essayistic prose that mix personal experience with quotation and references to art, philosophy, and history. The form – which prioritises accretive, fragmentary assemblages over essayistic synthesis – is recognisable as an inheritor of Roland Barthes's *Mourning Diary* or *Lover's Discourse* and can be found in many other contemporary prose works (such as Moyra Davey's *Index Cards* or Kate Zambreno's *Appendix Project*). Boyer's syntax, meanwhile, echoes the dispassionate quiet cultivated by Lydia Davis. But experimental poetry's capacities to estrange language and thereby denaturalise systems of power and exploitation remain part of the anti-capitalist *techne* of this mass-market book as well.

A lament for 'sororal death', *The Undying* is a polemic against cancer and the world that monetises it. It depicts Boyer's 'struggle to be a person who could think

---

[190] Hitchcock, 'An Interview'.   [191] King, 'Literature Is against Us'.

and write, … even if she thinks it makes her sick, even if she has to do in the negative, even if the only territory in which to think is that of the terrifying and too-generally-articulated *not–*'.[192] It is a book for life, staged not as a relentless effort to maintain positivity, but to disappoint the genetic and environmental fate that leads to illness: saying no to death rather than yes to life. Boyer has said that the book was written 'during periods of refusal', as a way of figuring out how 'to live as something more than information. I wanted to figure out some way to write what we need that wasn't going to turn it into a pornography of particularisation' – a risk that is associated both with memoir-writing, and with the conventions of the lyric 'I', seeking not to be devoured by an information economy that includes both digital and medical prolixity.[193] Earlier, Boyer described the 'refusal to be aware that something was wrong with my body. Even as I haemorrhaged, I wouldn't trust my own blood. Kidney stones were not. I mistook actual pregnancy for the hysterical kind'.[194] Sometimes, the refusal to admit illness is less a revolutionary act than a pattern of denial, rooted in family histories and poverty: 'Everyone knows that in the United States there is no budget for an uninsured mother's illness after the rent and food.'[195] Poverty makes it impossible to accede to the need for help, to risk a visit to the doctor, to lie down and be passive and withdraw labour. 'To admit weakness felt like a luxury belonging to someone else.' It is not always possible to refuse to be productive.

Boyer wrote the book so that others may 'feel less alone', offering a 'shared vocabulary for what we all our [*sic*] together and what they might someday face'.[196] Cancer emphasised her dependency and relatedness: it provoked a desire to reach 'outward toward love's shared reality' to form a crowd in the cancer pavilion.[197] But one of *The Undying*'s main themes is the peril of the singular. Boyer indicts the 'sickening world' where 'We were lonely, but unable to form the bonds necessary to end our loneliness. / We were overworked, but intoxicated by our own working' (*Undying* 19). Illness, like work and poverty, is profoundly isolating. The medical establishment treats 'everything as an individual experience as opposed to a collective, political one'. Being ill also displaces the expressivity of lyric with more prosaic needs. The intimacy of care work, care given and received, takes precedence over writing 'of love or its disappointments. Once treatment begins, my erotic longing is for assistive devices: a wheelchair and someone to push it, a bedpan and someone to empty it' (43).

---

[192] King, 'Literature Is against Us'.   [193] Ibid.

[194] Anne Boyer, 'We Who Can't Believe', *Wellcome Collection Blog* (11 June 2021): https://wellcomecollection.org/articles/YLeMJxAAACMAdIwp.

[195] Ibid.   [196] Olidort, 'Undying and Reparative Magic'.

[197] Anne Boyer, 'We Who Can't Believe'.

But this physical intimacy and desire for solidarity with those who suffer has an ambivalent relationship to the profoundly solitary experience of being a sick body. 'I was in this ideal situation in which I was getting a lot of love, and I still felt so alone and so desolate', Boyer has said.[198] Despite the best efforts of friends and their commitment to commoning, the ill person finds her body interposing its irreducible singularity between herself and other subjects who also suffer. Boyer speaks from 'this vast and common loneliness' (*Undying* 286). When a friend comments on a draft of *The Undying* that 'there is only intermittently any Us', she responds: 'I can't pretend to have felt less alone, as if swimming at the lake with my friends, then having swum past them, beyond the buoys, out in the deep where no one could come to rescue me and no one I loved had ever been' (285–6).

Her physical isolation is exacerbated by labour laws and precarity, which constrain the ability of kith to provide care. As a poor single mother, working a job 'where I was advised to never let on I was ill' (*Undying* 130), she is exposed to the dangers of a for-profit healthcare system in a country without statutory paid sick leave. Her need for care reveals the 'heterosexist and singlist assumptions of a state that doesn't provide any care for the sick, since it trusts that someone else (presumably a partner) will do it for free for the sake of a culturally constructed and legally sanctioned vision of love', as Laura De La Parra Fernández argues.[199]

> In the United States, if you aren't someone's child, parent, or spouse, the law allows no one else guaranteed leave from work to take care of you. If you are loved outside the enclosure of family, the law doesn't care how deeply – even with all the unofficialized love in the world enfolding you, if you need to be cared for by others, it must be in stolen slivers of time. (*Undying* 29)

The commoning of care is thwarted by legal and social structures that enforce the privations of privacy. As she navigates 'the catastrophe of needing care in a world in which single mothers are only meant to take care of everyone else', Boyer comes to understand why single, poor women are statistically at higher risk of dying from cancer. Her accounts of being sent home after a double mastectomy, or having to teach a class while still recovering from surgery, are vivid demonstrations of the health risks of being alone in a society that privileges the nuclear family above the 'extralegal and unofficial kind, unattached to the couple or family' (*Undying* 288).

---

[198] Hitchcock, 'An Interview'.

[199] Laura De La Parra Fernández, 'The Body's Unruly Event of Illness: (Re)orienting the Cancer Memoir in Anne Boyer's *The Undying*', *Prose Studies* 42.1 (January 2021): 34–52.

The Undying is not a lyric story of individuated, personal choices about love and relationships. It is a historical analysis of the conditions that reproduce medical inequality and isolate the sick from relation and the things they need to thrive. For Boyer, 'having a body in the world is not to have a body in truth: it's to have a body in history' (*Undying* 261). Ill people and their carers are 'marked by our historical particulars, constellated in a set of social and economic relations'; 'the history of illness is not the history of medicine – it's the history of the world – and the history of having a body could well be the history of what is done to most of us in the interest of the few' (30). Illness makes it difficult to think, but it does help her to think specifically about how the family, state, and medicine enforce privation. Behind the 'system of medicine' she finds 'all the other systems, family race work culture gender money education, and beyond those is a system that appears to include all the other systems, the system so total and overwhelming that we often mistake it for the world' (66).

These systems include the impact of environment and epigenetics on 'white supremacist capitalist patriarchy's ruinous carcinogenosphere' (*Undying* 78). In contemplating the links between cancer and environmental toxins, links that are also classed and racialised, Boyer considers the impact of a battery factory in her hometown, which 'releases lead through the winds and lands on and in everything: in the dogs that walk down the streets at dusk, in the catfish growing old in the beds of creeks, in the mosquitos and in the infants and schoolchildren and elderly, and in the workers at the factory, too' ('Heavy Air'). The list of human and more-than-human others affected by the contamination from the factory recalls Spahr's lists of chemicals in the water of the creek or the mother's breast milk, a 'pervasive dysfunction' Heather Houser names 'ecosickness': it 'links up the biomedical, environmental, social, and ethicopolitical' and reveals the 'imbrication of human and environment'.[200] While the resources of the enclosed commons are no longer freely accessible, everyone endures the contamination that leeches from the chemical commons.

Boyer's analysis returns us to Gilmore's definition of racism as 'the state-sanctioned or extralegal production and exploitation of group-differentiated vulnerability to premature death':[201] cancer is such a vulnerability, whose incidence and survival rates are impacted by race, class and gender. As such, it is not merely a personal misfortune but a political heuristic. It both mystifies and reveals. Chemicals used in chemotherapy damage her brain, reduce

---

[200] Heather Houser, *Ecosickness in Contemporary US Fiction: Environment and Affect* (New York, NY: Columbia University Press, 2014), 11.

[201] Gilmore, *Golden Gulag*, 28.

decision-making capacity, and hinder the ability to cognise the trauma of cancer and its treatments. But cancer also inducts the patient into an elaborate discursive regime in which she herself becomes a datum whose attributes she can barely comprehend. She is held in the 'cage of statistics' (*Undying* 18), while doctors 'read what my body has become: a patient made of information' (55). Her 'need to know' turns from her individual body, whose agonies she describes in terrible detail, towards the sociogenesis of illness and the 'historical particulars' of capitalism – while also resisting the translation of her specificity into a phenomenologically universalised body (208). The subjectivising resources of lyric can be deployed to resist this reduction to information. In that sense, *The Undying* attempts to raise the inner reality of the individual subject to 'a universal validity', and thus show how 'the poet's own subjective freedom ... flashes out in the struggle against the topic which is trying to master it', namely illness, and the capitalist structures that induce it.[202]

Having spent five years 'disabled with exhaustion and mental fog, and most of it in pain, mutilated', Boyer's desire to 'think about death outside of the cage of statistics' leads back to the calculus of poverty she explicates in *Garments*.[203] Survival 'cost a lot': 'I once had breasts, hair, sex hormones, a quick mind, vitality, a body I experienced as pleasure. Now I don't. To die, however, would have cost a lot, too, cost poems and books and adventures, cost my daughter her mother' (*Undying* 18). She discusses the environmental damage caused by the chemotherapy drugs, and their cost:

> The cost of one chemotherapy infusion was more money than I had then earned in any year of my life. . . . My problem is that I wanted to live millions of dollars' worth but could never then or now answer why I deserved the extravagance of this existence, why I consented to allow the marketplace to use as its bounty all of my profitable troubles. How many books, to pay back the world for my still existing, would I have to write? (86–7)

Her incalculable debt for her life reveals the absurdity of a capitalist economy of health and disease, and of debt, and the work we do to pay it, in general. Cancer and its treatment are not cessations of capitalist work, but its continuance, in practice and in logic. When she got cancer, 'I still worked a lot just now I finally really made money (for someone else)' (*Handbook* 174). Staying alive by becoming a 'hyper-consumer' of her expensive treatment produces profit for others. The condition intensifies the economic order she wants to overthrow: 'I have cancer, but that doesn't mean I don't have to work. I'm sick in *the inelastic*

---

202 Hegel, *Aesthetics*, 2:1111, 1142.
203 Anne Boyer, 'The Undying', *Mirabilary Substack* (13 September 2019): https://anne boyer.substack.com/p/the-undying.

present imperfect – the tense in which you have to pay rent for all of eternity' (*Handbook* 192).

Even the way cancer is discussed – as a pathological colonisation of the body by aggressive, proliferating cells – offers analogies to the capitalist order and its imperialist wars. As Susan Sontag argued, 'the language used to describe cancer evokes a different economic catastrophe: that of unregulated, abnormal, incoherent growth ... Cancer is described in images that sum up the negative behaviour of twentieth-century *homo economicus*', and treated with a 'counterattack' of violent medicines whose controlling metaphors are drawn from the language of warfare.[204] Similarly, Boyer describes cancer cells as 'aggressively looking for [the] immortality ... that is faithful to death'; 'their expansion – that wild, horrible living – has as its content only the emptiest death. "Like capitalism," I tell my friends, and mean, by capitalism, "life as we know it"' (*Handbook* 202). Illness radicalises her analysis of that life and makes the necessity of its overturning even more urgent.

Illness troubles understanding, damages the organs of knowledge, consumes all the energy that might be used for thought and creativity, and reduces a person to the bare attempt to survive. But it also offers a terrible capacity for revelation by deranging the senses and intensifying experience. 'It is only in sickness that space is deranged by new experience and sensation, and therefore presents itself as a fresh study', Boyer says.[205] *The Undying* takes up this key feature of disability writing, which Michael Davidson compares to the Russian Formalist trope of *ostrenenie* or 'laying bare the device': a literary technique of defamiliarisation that 'exposes the routinized, conventional ... character of daily existence'.[206] This is why, for Davidson, a 'poetics – as much as a politics – of disability is important: because it theorises the ways that poetry defamiliarises not only language but the body normalised within language' (118). Those effects are catalogued in *The Undying*: sickness

> vivifies the magnitude of the body's parts and systems. In the sickbed, the sick disassemble and this disassembly crowds a cosmos, organs and nerves and parts and aspects announcing themselves as unfurling particulars: a malfunctioning left tear duct – a new universe; a dying hair follicle – a solar system; that nerve ending in the fourth toe of the right foot – now eviscerating under chemotherapy drugs – a star about to collapse. (*Undying* 99)

---

[204] Susan Sontag, *Illness as Metaphor* (London: Penguin, [1977] 2002), 64–65.

[205] Alison Karasyk and Amelia Wallin, 'Conversation with Anne Boyer', *aCCeSSions*, https://ameliawallin.com/Anne-Boyer-in-conversation.

[206] Michael Davidson, *Concerto for the Left Hand: Disability and the Defamiliar Body* (Ann Arbor, MI: University of Michigan Press, 2008), 5.

Femi depicted the body as a series of houses; Boyer shows us a body becoming cosmos. Like John Donne's *Devotions upon Emergent Occasions*, which she cites, *The Undying* deploys geographic and astronomical metaphors for the suffering of the individual body. Poetry is ready to capture these estrangements, as time and spatial orientation are warped and language changed by illness.

Perhaps, rather than *ostranenie*, *The Undying* deploys its poetics of cancer as a version of the more politicised estrangements of the Brechtian *Verfremdungseffekt*, laying bare the toxic conditions of capitalist production both in its aetiology and its treatment. Eleni Stecopoulos argues that 'Healing, and perhaps embodiment itself, entails a certain estrangement or transform-ation, but also reintegration into culture.'[207] As such, illness stimulates critique; it is a *rite de passage* that begins by isolating the sufferer before (hopefully) returning them, renewed and full of the charisma of their transformation, to the community. For Stecopoulos, illness allows people to 'actually experience the poetics of their bodies' (48): a poetics in Boyer's case of the body's refusal, which is also 'an agile and capacious "for"' (Boyer, 'No', *Handbook* 16). Jim Ferris describes 'crip poetry' as full of 'possibility, the edgy potential, the openness and even likelihood of transformation ... in consciousness, not only the consciousness of the poet and the reader, but the potential to transform the world'.[208] Sheila Black names a similar force when she identifies disability poetry as 'inherently a poetry of liberation/revolution'.[209] For Black, disability poetics is 'a poetics of "negative capability" in all the ways John Keats may have intended it – an upheaval, a defamiliarisation, an ability to remain open'. Boyer has also argued that 'Politics, even more than poetry, requires an aptitude for a kind of negative capability, a kind of rigorous not-needing-to-know to know, like how by its very nature freedom is almost entirely unknowable from the condition of being unfree, and yet those who are unfree struggle for what they can't-yet-know every minute on this earth.'[210] Illness offers a lens for viewing 'the world right now, which we are always being told is ending, but which we wake up to each day, the no-future future that is always unfurling right before our eyes'.[211] The world appears to the sick person not as a distorted copy of the actually existing one, but in all its deranged pathology, and that leads to the 'undeniable challenge to revolutionise everything – yes, everything! – for the first time really and in the right way' (*Undying* 274).

---

[207] Eleni Stecopoulos, *Visceral Poetics* (Oakland, CA: ON Contemporary Practice, 2016), vii.

[208] Jim Ferris, 'Crip Poetry, or How I Learned to Love the Limp': https://wordgathering.syr.edu/past_issues/issue2/essay/ferris.html.

[209] 'Disability Poetics: A Conversation with Sheila Black', *Poetry International*: www.poetryinternationalonline.com/disability-poetics-conversation-with-sheila-black/.

[210] King, 'Literature Is against Us'.   [211] Olidort, 'Undying and Reparative Magic'.

The Undying thinks at the intersection of race, class, gender, ability, migration status, religion, and age, opening from the prostration of the sick body into an active engagement with the whole world. In sickness, 'what we once thought of as closed becomes opened, and our connection to everything else heightened, both what we give and receive'.[212] The wound is an image of that connection. Dennis Slattery argues that the wound is

> an opening where the self and the world may meet on new terms, perhaps violently, so that we are marked out and off, a territory assigned to us that is new, and which forever shifts our tracing in the world. . . . To be wounded is to be opened to the world; it is to be pushed off the straight, fixed, and predictable path of certainty and thrown into ambiguity, or onto the circuitous path, and into the unseen and unforeseen.[213]

That space of ambiguity and newness is one that experimental poetry like Boyer's has attempted to occupy, and describes also its dream of revolution. For Petra Kuppers, the scar 'moves matter into a future of a new flesh: a different subject emerges, a re-creation of the old into the new, into a repetition that holds on to its history even as it projects itself into an unpredictable future'.[214] Spahr acknowledged the body as a tiny, enclosed limit, which made it impossible to do more than press against the other, while ingesting involuntarily the poisons and remains of the dead every time we breathe. In Boyer's imagining, people open through their wounds into a heightened awareness of their relation to the world and each other, and the possibilities for a new future that is free from the ruin induced by 'white supremacist capitalist patriarchy'.

For Boyer, 'what we must find lies right there between the vulgas and the vulnus, the crowd and the wound' (*Handbook* 25). She argues that 'What we all do share are these experiences of loss, of pain, of disruption and devastation, and somewhere in the loss we can develop and become more deeply connected.'[215] Writing is one place where the sick can gather, in opposition to the privatisation of space, especially medicalised space. Imagining fantastic architectures such as a temple of weeping, 'castles for nervous laughter, grottos for the stultified, and yurts for burning shame' in her 'Formulary for a New Feeling', Boyer conceptualises different spaces for shared sentiment (*Handbook* 110, 112). These might include the poem. She proposes 'insubordinately sensitive publics', gathering 'for the systematic derangement of the

---

[212] Olidort, 'Undying and Reparative Magic'.

[213] Dennis Slattery, *The Wounded Body: Remembering the Markings of Flesh* (Albany, NY: SUNY Press, 2000), 7, 13.

[214] Petra Kuppers, *The Scar of Visibility: Medical Performances and Contemporary Art* (Minneapolis, MN: University of Minnesota Press, 2007), 19.

[215] Olidort, 'Undying and Reparative Magic'.

sensitivities' (*Handbook* 108) – extending Rimbaudian poetics to a collective project where the transfer of emotion among bodies 'will result in unmitigated restructuring of somatic and social life'. People will emerge from single-family dwellings and the work of dampening their feelings in those spaces, into a 'new order of common emotion' (*Handbook* 110). This is also a call to reimagine the privacy and privations of lyric intimacy as a commons where the individual heart could be handed on to the crowd.

In these restructured architectures and new orders of feeling, even the language of pain will be reinvented. Boyer records 'pain's leaky democracies' to remind us of 'our un-oneness' (*Undying* 239), a mutual dependence that recalls her love of the crowd and stadium thought experiment. *The Undying* contradicts Elaine Scarry's argument that pain destroys language: rather, Boyer says, it 'changes it'. The poets, marketplaces, and dictionaries may currently lack a language adequate to pain, but Boyer wonders if 'pain is widely declared inarticulate for the reason that we are not supposed to share a language for how we really feel' (*Undying* 213). Pain, illness, death, and language are not natural – they have histories, and 'the truth of history is also the truth of language and this is that everything will always change and soon. Every sensate body is a reminder that tomorrow is not today' (242). Operations to denaturalise or alter language, to expand its capacities for expression at the edge of the possible, might help us to 'share' more than just how we feel.

Lyric has long been associated with loss and ruin; so the book of the lost would be a lyric book. Written in common, it might change lyric and the experience of loss into something that is not only ordinary, but a site of struggle that leads towards the transformation of the world. Can books really do that? Boyer offers *The Undying* as 'a minor form of reparative magic', which might 'manifest the communism of the unlovable'. This book of the lost wants to regenerate people and their stricken body parts through its sentences: 'If I could write the earth into opening up I would, and bring back to life an insurgent army of the dead women, but I never learned to write well enough to do all of that' (*Undying* 284–5). No one has. Nonetheless, she refuses

> to watch us die of this ugly arrangement of the world without fighting back. If telling is the only talent I have, then I will tell . . . I can only hope to be enough of a poet that I can find a literary form that can repel some of these operations that would use the suffering of most of us for the profit of a few. Or if my experience is going to be absorbed, let it at least be like poison.[216]

Her books prove 'that we must force ourselves against ourselves to live, to see clearly and thus to see life, when death has put on his costume and gathered in so

---

[216] Karasyk and Wallin, 'Conversation'.

close around us'.[217] This is the ultimate refusal: to refuse death, and the planetary death drive that brings us to the brink of ruin, and to find a language for shared pain and its eventual overcoming.

Epilogue

This Element has explored the radical potential to be found in lyric tenderness. It is a kind of epilogue to the more pessimistic account I gave of the lyric in *Poetry and Bondage*. There, my focus was on the constraints that fasten to lyric personhood; on the way poetry has tracked slavery and carcerality over its long history, both really and metaphorically; and on the tendency of poetry, when most ambitious to imagine transcending materiality or to affirm the inalienable freedoms of human beings, to get snagged on the chains in which it imagines its unfree others to languish. Even if poetry never exceeded those constraints, it would still be worth writing, for the constraints are real. This book has attempted to imagine a different way to think with lyric.

I have, for many years, been preoccupied by poetry's negativities, while wanting to resist what Jacques Rancière describes as literature's misfortune: that it has 'only the language of written words at its disposal to stage myths of a writing beyond writing, everywhere inscribed in the flesh of things. This misfortune obliges it to the sceptical fortune of words that make believe that they are more than words and critique this claim themselves'.[218] That's why I said in the Introduction that poetry wishes to participate in the world's dissolution and repair – not that it effects those transformations. Nonetheless, this Element has argued, briefly and sometimes allusively, that lyric poetry has not retreated into the eternal present or vaporous private subject or dream of pure spirit: it is a powerful political form, capable of addressing the crises of capitalism, and arising from vividly shared experiences of the riot, strike, occupation, illness, and other moments when individuals discover themselves as a collective.[219] Naming this moment as a realisation of the commons, communing, or undercommons ('primarily characterised by the everyday practice of working and making in a (per)version of that old Greek sense of *poiesis*. It is a social poetics: a constant process where people make things and make one another or, to be more precise, where inseparable differences are continually

---

[217] Anne Boyer, 'We Who Can't Believe'.

[218] Jacques Rancière, *Mute Speech*, trans. James Swenson (New York, NY: Columbia University Press, 2011), 175.

[219] Jasper Bernes, 'Poetry and Revolution', in *After Marx: Literature, Theory, and Value in the Twenty-First Century*, ed. Colleen Lye and Christopher Nealon (Cambridge: Cambridge University Press, 2022), 240–252 (241, 247).

made', in Fred Moten's formulation[220]), the poems discussed here have found
the commons in the artistic, imaginative and tender life of the housing estate; the
songs of Non-Revolution; the border traced in peacock ore; and the cancer
pavilion. They find it in mourning rituals and performances of passivity. They
show their wounds, the ones that open them to chemical toxins, police inspection, and air. They look beyond the human individual towards planetary ecosystems teeming with an abundance of creatures, threats, and relations.[221]
Fantasising about the communisation of eros, their visions of social love are
also distinctly grounded in personal love: 'they', the familial plurality in Spahr's
poetry; 'mandem' as the collective who inhabit the endz and sustain each other
in Femi's; Kapil's nuclear family as allegory for the traumas of migration;
Boyer seeing in the crowd the traces of individual parenting care. Their work
provides some beautiful answers to Joshua Clover's questions: 'What does
a poetics of surplus populations look like?'; '*what will be adequate to this
moment?*'.[222] It is particularly valuable to me in showing how the individualised
lyric subject can expand beyond the privations of its own borders to become
a commons.

     Throughout this Element, I've meditated on the relationship between the
privileges of autonomy and subjectivity encoded in the lyric 'I', and the forms
of collectivity – the book of the lost – that might displace its liberal inwardness.
This is a question that preoccupies many contemporary poets. Sean Bonney
repeatedly returned to Rimbaud's dictum '*je est en autre*', which he read
through Kristin Ross's scholarship on the Paris Commune as pointing towards
'the transformation of the individual into the collective when it all kicks off'.[223]
Bonney dreamed of a poetry that could

> make visible whatever is forced into invisibility by police realism, where the
> lyric I – yeh, that thing – can be (1) an interrupter and (2) a collective, where
> direct speech and incomprehensibility are only possible as a synthesis that
> can bend ideas into and out of the limits of insurrectionism and illegalism.[224]

Speaking the enemy's language in the prosody of police batons, with punk
venom and tender hope, Bonney's poetry is dialectical: hate and love, clarity
and obscurity, unveiling truths and skulking in the margins of the surveilled

---

[220] Moten, *A Poetics of the Undercommons*, 24.
[221] On the figure of the commons in postwar and Romantic poetry, see Eltringham, *Poetry &
     Commons*.
[222] Joshua Clover and Chris Nealon, 'The Other Minimal Demand', in *Communism and Poetry:
     Writing against Capital*, ed. Ruth Jennison and Julian Murphet, 21–35 (34).
[223] Kristin Ross, *The Emergence of Social Space: Rimbaud and the Paris Commune* (London:
     Verso, 2015) and *Communal Luxury: The Political Imaginary of the Paris Commune* (London:
     Verso, 2018).
[224] Bonney, *Letters against the Firmament*, 141–142.

police state. He also knew that 'a rapid collectivising of subjectivity equally rapidly involves locked doors, barricades, self-definition through antagonism etc.' (140). The electrified grid's edgelessness would not be dismantled easily, nor can it be counteracted by catholic fantasies of the brotherhood of man.

Bonney is one of many poets whose efforts to imagine a collective lyric 'I', against despair, under the gathering storm of fascism and ecological disaster, make it possible for me not only to go on reading and thinking about poetry as a way of understanding the world, but to go on. Within the catastrophes of police violence, border securitisation, racism, oil spills, oil wars, privatisation, and extraction that these poetries grieve and rage, when it's easier to imagine the end of the world than the end of capitalism, there are many poets working hard to imagine the way *this* form of the world might end. They are doing it together, at poetry readings and performances, in magazines and small presses, in conversation, sustaining each other and hope.

Audre Lorde celebrates poetry's dark, ancient, and deep 'places of possibility within ourselves [that] are dark because they are ancient and hidden; they have survived and grown strong through darkness', the inchoate and the obscure as a site of creative potential and radical renewal. By contrast, Robert von Hallberg has described lyric as concerned with 'dark, lost causes' – and suggests that's a bad thing. For von Hallberg, 'Lyric poets have no reason to expect their art to transform the future, to right wrongs, or redeem loss. An expectation of failure, not triumph, is built into poems.'[225] I won't embrace that pessimism, even though the causes feel even more lost in 2023 than they did when he wrote in 2008. Rather, I believe that now, when (as Mark Fisher puts it) 'capitalism seamlessly occupies the horizon of the thinkable', poetry plucks at the unthinkable.[226] As Boyer argues, it does so precisely through its negativity. In the 'no', which is the defiant soul itself, we find 'the ingredient of the possible, including a possible literature and a possible world'.[227]

The ideas discussed in this Element are shared by many activists working to abolish the existing world. I wouldn't say that poetry is more effective than being in the streets: but poems have particular powers that we can turn towards the collective good. Those superpowers include the capacity to analyse complex relations and subjective experiences, to synthesise seemingly fragmentary or disparate facts and conditions and to show how they are implicated within the whole known as capitalism, to modulate between the particular and the general or the personal and the impersonal in ways that disavow attachment to individualism (even if a great deal of bad poetry clings to selfhood), to cross-

---

[225] Robert von Hallberg, *Lyric Powers* (Chicago, IL: University of Chicago Press, 2008), 13.

[226] Mark Fisher, *Capitalist Realism: Is There No Alternative?* (Winchester: Zer0 Books, 2009), 8.

[227] Goldstein, 'Find Something to Hide'.

reference the lack that is erotic love with the lack that is the world's insufficiency,[228] to activate the revolutionary pleasures of misunderstanding and not-yet-understanding, to condense, expand, and symbolise, to press into the gap between the imaginary object and the object that exceeds imagination, to be a present event while occupying the long unfoldings of history, to invite the reader to share an experience that changes each time the poem is encountered, to critique, dream, and startle the faculties of perception into a wakefulness that makes the world, suddenly and irreversibly, new. This is what good poetry can do. I am happy, after thirty years of writing and thinking about poetry (am I that old already?), to say so, and to hope for more, in the company of my contemporaries.

---

[228] More on this in Andrea Brady, 'The Determination of Love', *Journal of the British Academy* 5 (2018): 271–308.

Acknowledgements

I am grateful to Eric Falci for his advice and support, and to the anonymous readers of this manuscript for their suggestions. Much of this Element was written during a period of intensive industrial action in UK Higher Education, including strikes and a marking boycott. My employer responded to the latter with 113 days of punitive pay deductions. I am grateful for the solidarity of my trade union colleagues who literally paid my wages and fed my family during this period.

Quotations from *Poor* by Caleb Femi published by Penguin Press. Copyright © Caleb Femi, 2020. Reprinted by permission of Penguin Books Limited.

Cambridge Elements ☰

Poetry and Poetics

Eric Falci
University of California, Berkeley
Eric Falci is Professor of English at the University of California, Berkeley. He is the author of *Continuity and Change in Irish Poetry, 1966–2010* (2012), *The Cambridge Introduction to British Poetry, 1945–2010* (2015), and *The Value of Poetry* (2020). With Paige Reynolds, he is the co-editor of *Irish Literature in Transition, 1980–2020* (2020). His first book of poetry, *Late Along the Edgelands*, appeared in 2019.

About the Series
Cambridge Elements in Poetry and Poetics features expert accounts of poetry and poets across a broad field of historical periods, national and transnational traditions, linguistic and cultural contexts, and methodological approaches. Each volume offers distinctive approaches to poems, poets, institutions, concepts, and cultural conditions that have shaped the histories of poetic making.

Cambridge Elements ⁼

Poetry and Poetics

Printed in the United States
by Baker & Taylor Publisher Services